Mental Karate

Mental Karate

A Warrior's Guide

Tom Muzila

Bunk,
Continue your
strong practice!
Best,
Tom Muzila

EMPIRE Books

P.O. Box 491788, Los Angeles, CA 90049

First published in 2006 by Empire Books
Copyright © 2006 by Empire Books

First edition
06 05 04 03 02 01 00 99 98 97 1 3 5 7 9 10 8 6 4 2

Printed in the United States of America.

Empire Books
P.O. Box 491788
Los Angeles, CA 90049

Library of Congress: 2006009642
ISBN-10: 1-933901-01-2
ISBN-13: 978-1-933901-01-2

Library of Congress Cataloging-in-Publication Data

Muzila, Tom.
    Mental karate : a warrior' guide / By Tom Muzila. -- 1st ed.
        p. cm.
    Includes index.
    ISBN 1-933901-01-2 (pbk. : alk. paper)
    1. Karate--Psychological aspects. 2. Karate--Training.   I. Title.
    GV1114.3.M89 2006
    796.815'3019--dc22

2006009642

Prologue

I have been researching, studying and practicing warrior and athletic concepts, since the mid-1960s. Much of the information in this book has come directly from my own humble experiences, practices, study and opinions. The majority of information and experience in this topic has come from my karate teacher, Tsutomu Ohshima. He doesn't like to be referred to as master, but I and many other senior black belts and karate practitioners consider him a real master and true warrior. There are numerous true warriors, soldiers and athletes in the world, who have much more experience than I do. They survived situations, which truly defied all odds. I feel very humbled by some of the experiences and things they have accomplished and survived. I'm sure many of them used some similar concepts and philosophies to survive and attain their goals. I know they all have their own effective principles and concepts, which helped them to evolve their own higher consciousness. I'm sure many are much more extensive and articulated than what I have wrote about in this book. I would also recommend studying other serious warriors, soldiers and athletes. Discover what their insights and experiences were to achieve a higher level mentality and mind-set for fighting and combat.

—Tom Muzila

Dedication

This book is dedicated to all the warriors in human history who sacrificed their lives to make a positive evolutionary difference for the mental, technical and spiritual growth of mankind.

These men and women exhibited a warrior consciousness throughout their lives to make it better for the rest.

They fought for truth, honor, justice and benevolence their entire lives.

These individuals expected nothing in return for their efforts. They existed is all facets of life, throughout all periods of time.

These individuals expressed and exhibited a true warrior mentality. This warrior mentality gave them the fiery spirit to make a difference in life.

We all have the capacity to tap into this warrior consciousness to accomplish our dreams and to make life on earth better for all of us.

Acknowledgments

I would like to take a moment to acknowledge and thank all the individuals in my life who have inspired and motivated me to write this book. These individual's lives were great examples of what they believed in. They lived their lives by these unique concepts. I am in deeply grateful to my parents, Paul and Stella Muzila. They always inspired me to accomplish my dreams in the most positive way. My parents have been an excellent example of a positive, happily married couple.

Tsutomu Ohshima was a major influence in my life on every level. He inspired and encouraged me to face and challenge myself in every realm of my consciousness. His example compelled me to acquire an understanding of the mentality of these ancient warriors. I have attempted to live my own life by many of these warrior principles. I want to thank all my friends, seniors and students who always inspired me to push myself harder and farther. People such as Don Depree, Ken Osborne, Caylor Adkins, Greg Scott, Bob Lopez, Bill Ungerman, Frank Cole, Peter Guttilla and David LaManno.

These are just a few. There have been many others. I would also like to thank the entire Shotokan Karate of America Association and members for giving me many life-long friends, opponents and challenges.

I want to give special thanks to my in-laws, Dr. James Caron and Ethel Caron. They have continually supported my ideals, philosophies and principles. They also encouraged me to materialize these concepts in a book. This book would not have been possible without their help. I would also like to thank the entire Caron family, who have always strongly supported my endeavors.

Most importantly, I wish to thank my wife, Susan, and our two children, Kasha and Kayden. They have been the greatest support and inspiration in my life. I am continually attempting to

pass these concepts down to our own children. Susan has continuously supported me and encouraged me to follow my
dreams and ideals. Her dedication and support to our children
and me is a true example of a warrior's spirit and an inspiration
to others.

I thank all of you from the bottom of my heart.

Foreword

The answer to living life . . . *MENTALITY!* This book has the answers to gaining your maximum ability to accomplish things you thought impossible. We all have untapped mental strength. Self defeat is unjustly caused by a lack of confidence.

No matter how well we prepare ourselves through training and practice it all comes down to self at that moment, the control of our mind. Each person has depth and strength but are we capable of channeling it in the right direction. We need to corral our scattered thoughts and condense them, focus. Acquire ancient ideas and the mentality of Bushido, the way of the warrior and transform them to modern times. Many have to train rigorously to acquire it. There are just a few who have evolved this warrior mentality to its highest degree. The ancient warriors took the fear of death out of their everyday life and focused on their mission. This mentality will benefit every area of your life.

The true meaning and spirit of Karate-Do is revealed in every chapter.

Do you want to change you life, achieve success? This book will show you the way to apply ancient mentality along with its tactics, principles and techniques to your daily life. Fascinating true short stories give examples of what can be achieved when you manifest the warrior mentality.

If you are serious about improving all aspects of your life, you must read this book!

—Ken Osborne
Godan—Shotokan Karate of America

CONTENTS

Preface 1

Introduction 3

About the Author 4

Tsutomu Ohshima: A True Warrior Mentality 9

Esoteric Learning Methods 15

Chapter 1: Facing Yourself 33

Chapter 2: A Warrior Never Gives Up 41

Chapter 3: The Secrets of Firewalking 45

Chapter 4: Eliminate Fears in the Martial Arts 51

Chapter 5: Special Training 57

Chapter 6: The Power of Belief 67

Chapter 7: Mental Conditioning and Non-attachment 73

Chapter 8: Controlling Thoughts 81

Chapter 9: Positive Self-Controlling Attitude 91

Chapter 10: Unyielding Self-Confidence 101

Chapter 11: Developing Focus and Mental Strength 107

Chapter 12: Dynamic Imagery and Visualization 117

Chapter 13: Optimum Peak Performance Mental States 127

Chapter 14: Combat Mentality 137

Chapter 15: High-Powered Breathing Techniques for Inner Power 153

Chapter 16: Powerful Ki, Chi Generating Principles 167

Chapter 17: The Creativity of Perceptions Using them to Evolve Consciousness 175

Chapter 18: Develop Effective Practical Intuition 187

Chapter 19: Manifest Unlimited Creative Consciousness 199

Conclusion 205

Preface

The majority of books are written in the category of fiction or non-fiction. This book is neither and both at the same time. This book will cover the whole spectrum of learning, if it is read with the proper state of mind. It will stimulate your left brain (logical, rational) and your right brain (emotional, creative, intuitive). The material in the book will take you through various mental states, such as from beta, alpha, theta to delta. Most non-fiction books are written from a knowledge point of view. Fiction books are written from more of an emotional perspective. This book is written to discover, explore, express and expand more of an internal experience. When you read this book with the right state of mind and focus, it will stimulate and move your subconscious mind at the deepest levels. It will give you incredible insights, realizations and enlightenments in your life, which you can use to better understand and learn anything. It will give you the power to accomplish your dreams. You will acquire the fire in your spirit to penetrate and solve any problem or obstacle in your life. You will also learn how to harmonize any situation through the proper state of mind. Your mind will expand and you will discover that your mind is able to think much more laterally than linearly and this will broaden your capacity of understanding. This book is not concerned with learning and remembering information. It is focused on experiencing and remembering yourself, who you are at the deepest level and forging your mind to grow to unlimited capacities.

You are on your way to a self-empowering internal journey.

Introduction

The warrior spirit has been incredibly prevalent throughout history. Anytime a positive difference was accomplished in the evolution of the human race, it could always be attributed to the warrior spirit. We all have this warrior spirit within us. It doesn't matter what nationality, gender or race we are. Of course, the warrior spirit can be used for negative, selfish purposes, too. It all depends on the consciousness from which it is executed. We are going to deal with the most positive consciousness of the human spirit. The warrior spirit that is more selfless, compassionate and focused toward the betterment of a person and mankind. An excellent example of this true warrior spirit was executed on every level after the terrorist attack of the New York Trade Towers. Numerous people sacrificed their own lives to save others. True warriors have continuously sacrificed themselves throughout history. They are not only the fighting type of warriors, but they come from all walks of life and professions.

About the Author

Tom Muzila is one of the most appropriate individuals to teach and speak on these topics, concepts and principles. He has challenged the human spirit numerous times ... beyond all mental and physical limitations. He has accomplished many mental and physical feats that were thought to be next to impossible. He has proven that with proper spirit, conditioning and technical training, anything can be achieved. He is also considered one of the best karate and martial arts teachers around. Muzila has trained with the legendary karate master Tsutomu Ohshima for most of his life. He has taught and practiced karate and the martial arts for close to 40 years. Muzila has devoted his entire life to studying, researching and practicing optimum peak performance mental concepts and mind-over-matter accomplishments.

Muzila is a 5th-degree black belt in Shotokan karate, but he has practiced numerous martial arts, various fighting styles and boxing. He has participated on the U.S. Shotokan Karate Team. He holds many karate athletic world records, which exhibit incredible physical, mental stamina and endurance, one of which is practicing karate techniques for 24 hours straight. He has punched and kicked 10,000 times in one session on many

Tom Muzila attempting to pull as F-16 Fighter Jet, at Hill's Airforce Base in Utah.

numerous occasions. He has participated in, led and gone through 95 karate special training sessions. He also completed a 21-day karate special training, which encompassed training about 10 hours a day for 21 days. He has specialized in utilizing internal energy (chi or ki) exercises through the years to help accomplish many of the long endurance karate feats.

Muzila has been an avid mountain climber. Years ago, he climbed six mountains in the Pacific Northwest in seven days. He has walked barefoot over a pit of red-hot burning coals more than 100 times without getting burned or injured. He's squatted with an eight-pound iron ball 10,000 times, which took more than two and one half-hours. He has stood in a karate horse stance for three hours straight. Muzila has pulled 20,000 pound diesel trucks and an F-16 Air Force fighter jet using his principles. He has also run 50 miles and 25 miles on many occasions.

In the military, Muzila served in the U.S. Army Special Forces (Green Berets). He attended and graduated from some of the toughest military elite survival schools, such as airborne, ranger, jungle warfare, mountaineering, light and heavy weapons, pathfinder, desert and cold weather survival, sniper, scuba, visual tracking, HALO, ski school and numerous others. He has studied covert operations extensively. He also has studied instinctive combat shooting concepts for many years.

Muzila has extensive experience in executive protection and professional bodyguarding. He has been active in the field for more than 30 years and has specialized in celebrity protection.

Tom Muzila while in the U.S. Army Special Forces,
going through Jungle Expert Training School in Panama.

Tom Muzila punching, connected to a diesel truck, to better practice getting his hips in on a technique.

He has protected hundreds of celebrities, diplomats, dignitaries and their families in the world. He is an action and military advisor and also a stunt and fight coordinator for numerous feature films. He has trained many actors in physical conditioning and fighting techniques for lead parts. Muzila has taught numerous law enforcement agencies and elite military units in various subjects. He has also coached and trained some of the best athletes in the world in optimum peak performance mental states and the warrior mentality. He has a degree in Asian Religions and has specialized in researching parapsychological techniques as applied to success and achievement in life.

Tsutomu Ohshima:
A True Warrior Mentality

Tsutomu Ohshima is one of the rare individuals I have met whose consciousness embodies the concepts and insights of the ideal warrior mentality. He is an uncommon example of the contemporary warrior saint. He has always been ready to put his life and being down for truth and justice. He has dedicated his life to raising the awareness, strength and consciousness of human beings, and he has never wavered from this path. He has always made the evolution of higher consciousness and mentality first priority in his life. He is one of the very few top experts and masters of karate and martial arts on the planet.

Tsutomu Ohshima was born August 6, 1930. His career in the martial arts began with sumo at age five and continued with kendo and judo from ages seven until 15. He entered Waseda University, one of the most prestigious colleges in Japan, in 1948 and began practicing with Gichin Funakoshi, who was head instructor. Gichin Funakoshi is now considered the "Father of Modern Day Karate." He was responsible for popularizing karate to the entire world. There were many notable karate experts who practiced originally with Funakoshi, such as Egami, Obata, Kamata, Okuyama and Otsuka. Ohshima was responsible for bringing all of these seniors to the United States for us to practice with.

In 1961, Tsutomu Ohshima visited France and influenced many juniors to eventually start France Shotokan. Ohshima became captain of the Waseda University Karate Team in 1952. The same year he and some university friends developed tournament match rules to better protect the participates. It shortly became very popularly and widespread in the karate communities. In 1955, he decided to attend university and acquire a degree in America. He lived in Southern California and attended school there. Gichin Funakoshi granted him the rank of sandan (3rd-degree black belt) before he left Japan. The 3rd-degree black belt was the highest technical level degree at this time. Ohshima was given the degree of godan (5th-degree black belt) in 1959. It was the highest rank given in the original traditional karate system.

Ohshima started teaching traditional Shotokan karate in Southern California in 1955. A year later he started and formed the Southern California Karate Association. Karate started becoming popular in America and numerous people sought Ohshima to train with him. In 1974, he organized the national Shotokan Karate of America association. He has also started affiliate karate organizations in 15 different countries. His earlier karate groups and associations kept and still keep a close connection with Gichin Funakoshi's original principles and concepts. In 1967, Ohshima was the first senior karate teacher to organize and bring the first U.S. karate teams to compete against the Japanese teams. He has organized numerous karate teams throughout the years to participate in international events. Ohshima has led a number of international exchange practices and tournaments to help unite the world of traditional karate.

Ohshima was also the only one given personal permission from Gichin Funakoshi's family to translate his original book, "Karate-Do Kyohan." It was first published in English in 1973. Today, Ohshima is still giving direction, inspiration and encouragement to individuals and karate groups all over the world.

When Ohshima originally came to America, he was impressed by the incredible spirit he saw in the American young. His character and charisma naturally attracted numerous people to train with him. He was approached consistently to teach karate in many areas. Individuals eventually came from all over the world to train with him. Ohshima decided to stay in America and teach his ancient warrior philosophy and use this location for a central headquarters. He is one of the very few authentic individuals still keeping these ancient warrior secrets alive today. In my opinion and many other senior black belts, he is a perfect example of the ultimate warrior, balanced with a saint consciousness.

Gratitude to Tsutomu Ohshima

I would like to thank Tsutomu Ohshima, on behalf of his students, juniors, seniors, instructors, teachers and myself. He has made an incredible personal sacrifice his entire life to help keep these ancient warrior concepts alive. He does not look at it this way though. It is in his nature to automatically be this way. He made this his personal mission in life and has accomplished it and continues to do so. He does not do any of this to be thanked or appreciated. His consciousness is balanced, between an incredibly strong independent warrior mentality and being an extremely

Tsutomu Ohshima displaying extremely intense eye focus, while facing an opponent in Paris, France.

humble gracious human being. He has taught or touched, at least, a couple million people throughout his life. Those two million people have compounded his teachings to 10 times the number of the people who have been touched by his insights. Everyone he has touched throughout his life will admit that his teachings have had a profound positive affect on their lives. In my

Tsutomu Ohshima continuing to demonstrate that he has already beat his opponent mentally, before his opponent has attacked.

humble opinion, there are very few people on the planet who are the total embodiment of a warrior saint. Tsutomu Ohshima is one of those rare souls and human beings. The essence of the ancient warrior would not exist to the degree it does today if it were not for his life and teachings.

He continues to motivate and inspire me to stay true to the warrior's path and life. He has always had a profound effect on my life, and on my important decision for many years. I know that thousands of others would say the same. They have in turn taught his teachings throughout the world in many different countries. His teachings go beyond politics, religion, nationality, race and culture. They are to everyone's benefit. We have karate groups in Israel and Morocco. This is a good example because it is normally very hard for individuals in these two countries to get along. Through Ohshima's teachings, our karate members of these countries have been able to get along beyond politics and reli-

Tsutomu Ohshima hosted the first U.S.A.-Japan, Exchange Practice in 1967.

gion. They have acquired a much deeper meaning and understanding of life and are more willing to accept and understand each other. This is an example of the power of Ohshima's teachings. They connect us back to our original souls, as human beings here on this planet. He has dedicated his life to help others acquire a better understanding of themselves and life. His philosophy is based upon the ancient warrior's ideals. The majority of them are all exemplified in the warrior concepts included this book.

Ohshima's travels continually take him throughout the world, spreading the essence of these ancient warrior concepts and teachings. He has originated and started karate and martial art groups in numerous countries. He has always attracted the best quality people to his groups. He has never been concerned with quantity of people, only quality of people's mentality and consciousness in his organizations. He has never been interested in commercializing or franchising his teachings. Rather, his aim has always been to awaken others through our practice. We would like to thank him again for his continued teachings throughout the world and keeping these ancient warrior secrets alive today in this modern day society.

Esoteric Learning Methods

The Eastern method of learning leans toward a more esoteric approach. The Western mind depends more on the external method. It emphasizes more learned intelligent knowledge. Westerners read, learn, study, memorize information and attempt to experience the majority of things in life externally. For example, the typical way for college student, to learn is by reading books and magazines, and studying research material. They also listen to countless hours of lecture material. The mental Eastern approach is to attempt to experience truth and reality from deep within yourself. To experience that you must attempt to acquire the appropriate mentality to be able to recognize what truth is inside of us.

The esoteric Eastern approach is mainly from within. The more we can understand ourselves, the more we can understand others and the world we live in, including the universe. The Western student depends more on learning or studying the answers and having them told to him. The original esoteric student emphasizes the concept of being asked a question by a senior or a teacher and going off and contemplating the answer from within. The student would first attempt to acquire the appropriate mentality to contemplate the answer. He would then be more able to discover the answer from a deep internal source. The answer may come up quietly or it may take months or even years to arise from his subconscious mind. If we acquire a certain core of understanding about ourselves, we are more apt to relate that understanding to the world around us. That is, if we can learn to communicate with the deepest parts of our minds.

The person utilizing this esoteric method naturally activates a bigger capacity of his mind. Most people are familiar with the right and left brain concepts, which have been popularized the last few years. The esoteric method engages more of the right brain during a learning experience. The right brain governs the creative, imaginative, feeling and intuitive portion of the mind. Most Western-mentality individuals are trained more to develop the left brain. This part of the brain controls logic, rational and intelligence. Ideally, it would be best to be able to utilize the synchronization of both brains. This would be especially effective when trying to solve a specific problem, utilizing the benefits of both brains. You can see how this would be more advantageous in all aspects of life for us.

This is why in ancient—and even today in modern times—serious monks who lived many years in monasteries would be so respected. They would live in a monastery for 10, 15 or 20 years and have a better understanding of life than someone who had traveled extensively around the world. The concepts you will be reading in this book are written and based on these esoteric learning methods and principles. Of course, today in most societies, Eastern and Western, modern sophisticated knowledge through the Internet has taken over. The advantage is that it brings the exterior knowledge of the entire world closer together. The ancient tradition esoteric methods are slowly being lost today in this modern society and this is a great loss. I also feel these ancient traditional methods could be a great benefit to our modern world on every level.

This Book Is An Experience

This book is not based on the Western concept of learning. You do not have to memorize data or specific information and material. When you learn and memorize information, you are activating more of your left brain. As mentioned, this again is the part of your brain that governs the logical, rational and intellectual aspects of your mind. When you study or learn in this fashion, you broaden your information and expand your basic knowledge. This method will not change the deep part of your subconscious mind and the essence of your being. The warrior concepts have the capacity to do this, depending on the state of mind that you are in when you read the book.

If you read the chapters and concepts with an open mind, they can really change you at the deepest level of your subconscious mind. They will broaden your personal internal and external universe. The warrior concepts can help you see, experience and understand the true essence of reality. This subconscious exposure to these concepts will expand your philosophical understanding of the world and other dimensions. Your subconscious mind will automatically contemplate and digest the meaning of the maxims over a period of time. The concepts are written in a way for you to actually experience them. If you understand one warrior concept, you can expand your whole belief system. The warrior concepts are organized to make you contemplate and meditate on them throughout the day. If you go to sleep with a warrior principle on your mind, you may awake in the morning with a new realization. Warrior concepts will naturally be associated to specific experiences in life and you will continually acquire new insights in life.

Relating the concepts to experiences in life will naturally assist you in facing fears, insecurities and mental blocks. This occurs without you even realizing it. When you acquire the warrior mentality, you replace mental blocks with a much deeper understanding and life. That understanding will expose a much deeper core of your inner self. A much stronger inner self will arise within you. You will tap into the meaning and understanding of the warrior's mind, as you go through various experiences in your day. Eventually, various elements from each concept will slowly connect and relate to each other. You will acquire a new level of understanding. It doesn't matter whether the warrior concepts are simple, complex or contradictory to your rational mind. In time, you will see how they are all connected. If you read and study this book with the right attitude, it will teach you to think more laterally. This insight and realization will help you relate this to numerous issues in life.

Appreciation of Individuals Who Made a Difference

This book is written in appreciation to all individuals who sacrificed their own lives to make a positive difference for the evolution of mankind. These people are not in abundance, but they have existed since the birth of the human race. The number of these people throughout history is equal to a very small percentage, but their selfless influence to the human race is equivalent to hundreds of thousands. These individuals utilized the warrior mentality to benefit the masses on every level. They have done this from the being of the human race and they will continue to benefit humanity through history.

These people sacrificed themselves, mentally, physically and emotionally for the benefit of all. They all accepted the challenge to attempt to forge a better path or life for everyone. These individuals faced themselves on every level. They faced their fears, weaknesses, insecurities and mental blocks to accomplish their missions. These men and women have existed in all eras of history. They have been involved and specialized in every type of profession, art or specialty. They were leaders, discoverers, explorers, researchers, adventurers, warriors, soldiers, ministers, saints, monks, doctors, scientists, masters of arts and professional experts in every specialty. Numerous fathers and mothers also are included in this elite category. The list goes on. It occupies almost every race, nationality, religion and political state. These are people who have sacrificed themselves to inspire and motivate others to personally evolve and push themselves farther and harder to achieve a higher level mentality. It was these people who were responsible for most of the discoveries made in science and technology for the benefit of the human race. They aided mankind in developing a higher consciousness in all facets of the sciences, including human psychology and health. They continually keep themselves on the cutting edge of challenges so everyone can benefit. Their mission is to fight for freedom and the liberation of consciousness.

They sacrifice themselves to help raise the caliber of goodness for the whole human race. Throughout history, there were

Tom Muzila meditating in the Sierra Nevada mountain's in California.

legions of soldiers and warriors who also sacrificed their lives for the benefit of peace and justice in the world. Numerous philosophers and researchers have studied a multitude of subjects and wrote thousands of books to pass knowledge down to benefit the many.

These people had no limits or boundaries in their minds. Their mission in life was much bigger than any fear, insecurity or mental block they had. If a weakness arose in their minds, they were able to face it, deal with it and extinguish it from their mentality to accomplish their mission. They knew how to use their will and discipline to be able to penetrate any obstacle they were confronted with. All of these people knew how to use and generate their warrior mentality and use it effectively in life. As I mentioned, this book is intended to show appreciation for all of these individuals throughout history who used their warrior mentality to make a positive difference for everyone. They sacrificed themselves so every human being could have more freedom and a better opportunity to evolve and grow mentally. They will not be forgotten ... past, present or future. This warrior mentality and spirit is responsible for maintaining peace, harmony and justice on our planet. As long as these warrior mentality individuals exist, happiness, freedom and peace will always continue to exist.

Why Focus on a Warrior Mentality?

Why is the focus of the book on the warrior mentality? Majorities of people are conditioned to think warriors are aggressive and only want to fight or wage war. This might be true for the lower mentality thugs and fighters, but it is not so for the true warriors. The higher the level of consciousness a warrior is the more he or she wants to fight for peace and the benefit of all. They only fight when it is absolutely necessary, and in most cases, it is not for their own personal benefit. Their mission is ultimately peace, harmony, tranquility and justice for everyone.

We have four major elements in the mind of man; they have existed throughout the entire history of the human race and they have really contributed to make a difference. They are very simple, yet very powerful, depending how we expressed them. These elements have determined the destiny of mankind in one way or another. I am referring to being positive, negative and expressing strength or weakness.

We either have positive people expressing strength, while being in control, or negative people expressing strength, while being in control. These basic elements usually will determine the outcome in any situation. Positive people exude their activities for the benefit of all and negative individuals focus more on their own selfish purpose in life. A vast gray area can exist between both of these attitudes. There are an endless number of combination possibilities in that area, too.

An individual attempting to live up to a higher purpose in life can get confused at times. Yet the true warrior is always decisive.

He or she knows when to fight and when to harmonize with a situation in life. People who have important positions influence the majority of the public using these four major elements in many different ways. This majority is controlled in organized politics and religions, but also in the realm of ideals, concepts and principles of life. The media can influence a major portion of society. Previous culture and habits will also influence many people. True warriors will not be influenced by these factors. They will face themselves at an inner level in their minds and challenge themselves to improve their mentality throughout their lives. We must all learn to live as individuals and not let ourselves be influenced negatively by society. The true warrior must learn to be guided by his inner core self. If someone has trained himself to face himself on every level, he should have developed an inner centered and balanced inner self to be guided by.

We all have a tremendous power within us. That inner strength is willed through our warrior mentality. We have the ability to tap into it and activate it anytime we wish. The more we use and activate our warrior mentality the easier it is to tap into and use it for any situation we desire. That warrior mentality has an enormous ability, which is beyond comprehension. We don't always realize it, but we are constantly having an internal or external battle with some aspect of our own lives. We are continuously striving for some goal, which we must sometimes fight to acquire. Most people are having a constant struggle within themselves. Their conscious and subconscious minds are in contradiction. We are struggling and battling in our relationships, our jobs, professions and positions, and our personal and family finances. There are struggles in religions and politics, which we have to deal with and be mentally strong all the time. When we activate our warrior spirit, we can rise above the struggles of life. The more we are balanced and centered in our core, the more advantage the warrior spirit can be to us. The key to activating the warrior spirit is taking the right or best action or choice in a certain situation in life. It is always better to have the foresight and knowledge to

Tom Muzila using an old judo training hip practice, against a pine tree in the Sierra mountains in Northern California.

avoid a negative situation in the first place. There is a secret formula that will help guarantee your success when you do have to fight and do battle in life. The secret exists within the essences of these warrior concepts and principles.

The warrior does not have to fight all the time. The majority of the time it is better to surrender and harmonize with the situation. This approach can win for us, a number of battles without a fight, and many times exemplifies life on a higher plane. We can make any experience a positive one, if we face it with the appropriate mentality and attitude. There are many reasons we experience or even create specific situations in our lives. Subconsciously, we create and put ourselves in these situations to evolve and work on some deeper element inside of us. We have the freedom to learn and evolve from every situation in life, positive or negative. We are totally responsible for that, we make the choice.

When an individual wants to learn to be stronger and face his insecurities, he must learn to have strict eyes on himself. He must first learn to criticize himself before he criticizes others. He must face all of his weaknesses, fears, insecurities, and mental blocks and extinguish them from his consciousness. It is a continuous battle to acquire a higher state of mind and evolve. There is always a price to pay you have to consciously make the choice to sacrifice. We all need more understanding, enlightenment and harmony to make our planet a better place for all of us.

This warrior mentality holds the secret concepts and principles of life. Many have been created, or rephrased from ideas taken from numerous great and enlightened individuals throughout history. Each generation must find its own voice. If you read and study them with the right mentality, you will learn how to acquire great mental strength and fortitude. Of course, you have to constantly apply them to real life situations. You will understand how to live your life in total harmony ... internally and externally. If you apply these concepts continuously, you will acquire a strong will and understand how to use and not use discipline wisely in your life. You will discover true spirituality and peace of mind in life. These warrior concepts contain the knowledge our deeper minds, inner selves and spirit crave.

The Warrior Within Us

Everyone has the potential to tap into and develop a warrior mentality. Some people seem naturally born with it and others have to train and practice intensely to achieve it. It's dormant in individuals who haven't activated and groomed it. The warrior mentality can be quite advantageous in specific situations when properly used. We have the ability to tap into and utilize it throughout our entire lives, but it does take constant intense practice and training to really learn how to activate it. The warrior state of mind gives you ample focus and concentration to accomplish what you may have once thought was impossible. It will keep you balanced and focused on your path and what you should be continually striving for.

The warrior concepts contain all the necessary knowledge and mental information to stimulate the warrior spirit and its expression. It's especially important when life seems difficult or stressed. Achieving a warrior's state of mind will assist you to become more successful in everything you do. Through consistent practice, you will train a certain part of your mind to actually be a warrior.

True warriors only fight as a last resort and when there are no other options. They only draw their sword when it is absolutely necessary. They never draw or brandish their sword to show off. When true warriors actually draw their sword, it means to the death. Their primary mission is to help acquire peace, harmony and justice in life.

Practical Positive Results of This Mentality

The Japanese were totally crushed after World War II. They were devastated and most of them thought they would never recover. Their cities and economy were largely destroyed from fire and bombing, which were from the effects of the bomb. Yet, it is interesting how quickly and strongly Japan came back to become a big economic power. As it happened, Edwards Deming, the economist philosopher, an American warrior largely ignored in his own country, offered advice that many Japanese business leaders took to heart. The older generation of people, feel the real factor in bringing Japan totally back from widespread destruction were these ancient samurai philosophies. They were able to tap back into their ancient warrior principles to come back from this horrendous collapse. They used warrior concepts and strategies, talked about in this book.

For hundreds of years, the samurai were steeped in these precepts, principles and ancient codes. Japan was a feudal country for more than a thousand years. Its lords and soldiers were well experienced in battle and life-or-death situations. They learned which mental concepts and methods worked and which ones did not work. It was very interesting, because they found the principles they acted pm when facing, death in a combat situation, also worked in a life situations. Most of these true warriors and samurai had faced death many times in combat. Their mental techniques were proven, because if they didn't work, they would die. This method was very effective, because without a doubt, they knew the best mentality to have in a crisis situation. Many of the older generation of Japan remembered these ancient sources and knew how powerful they were. The majority of these principals were used to mentally rebuild Japan to the nation it is today. These techniques were used in helping to rebuild their businesses, companies and corporations. The most important point is that the Japanese culture passed down from feudal times through the Shogunate and the Meiji period remained largely intact, with the Emperor a somewhat reduced figure. This provided a source of strength to the people they used to redevelop the mentality of the Japanese people. These concepts and methods inspired them to bring their country back to a major economic power in the world today.

American corporate executives started doing some serious negotiating in trade and economics with Japanese executives in the early 1980s. Originally, the Americans had a difficult time, because the Japanese would never show their intentions, but remain patient. Americans were upfront with their position on specific issues and it was obvious to the Japanese where the Americans were coming from. The Japanese would always do the opposite and wouldn't telegraph their position on certain issues. This confused the Americans and made their negotiating difficult. The Japanese were using many of the concepts and techniques hidden within these warrior concepts. Many Eastern philosophy books were written at this time and they became very popular among American corporate executives. Most of the popular books specialized on ancient topics related to warfare. They covered battle strategy, concepts, principles and techniques. The executives read and studied them and eventually became much more familiar with the Japanese culture, history and mentality. As the Americans became more educated in these topics, their negotiations with the Japanese became easier. They were able to create a more beneficial position to both sides, and that became a win-win situation. Many corporate executives in America started making these books a required reading for their business executives. When this happened, the total relationship between Japan and America became very beneficial to the world. Two of these books that were popular were "Sun Tsu, The Art of War" and "The Book of Five Rings" by Miyamoto Musashi, considered one of the best samurai in Japanese history.

The most recent incident that really expressed and emphasized this warrior spirit was horrific tragedy on September 11, 2001. The human mind can exhibit incredible spirit under any circumstances, especially when it is trained and programmed that way. The human spirit, which signifies liberated freedom and spirit, was still able to be activated and express itself, even with so much devastation. This is a perfect example to show how powerful the human mind is. We have programmed and trained our minds in America to exhibit the spirit of strength and freedom. The American spirit was able to rise and come back even after that most terrible experience. This warrior's liberated spirit has no limits, even when the odds are heavily against us. All we have to do is realize and believe it in the deepest part of our hearts and minds. This warrior spirit is the most powerful element and energy on the planet. Nothing can conquer it when expressed with the proper mentality and consciousness. It is totally limitless and boundless.

Through the years, there have been countless countries and nations that have utilized this warrior spirit to develop their souls for the good of everyone. These nations have used their highest-level warriors to achieve the best for their nation and the best for mankind. There are stories of samurai who had a cliff to their back and had to face an army of 10,000 by themselves. It would logically seem like all odds were against them and it was impossible to succeed under the great odds against them. The stories state that if the warrior had the right mentality and spirit, no matter what the odds, this mentality and spirit of righteousness could activate a miracle. Somehow, the universe or God would provide a way for this one true warrior to defeat this army of 10,000,

Tom Muzila executing thousands of punching techniques in the ocean at a Karate Special Training in Long Beach.

which goes against all common experience.. This mentality and spirit could change an impossible situation to a possible situation.

You can see how these philosophies can benefit a nation as a whole? Can you imagine what they can do for you?

Opportunity to Activate the Warrior Mentality

This is a very critical time on our planet. Many things are shifting and changing radically and quickly. Some of these changes are moving at the speed of light. The next 10 or 20 years are going to be a sensitive time for everyone on the planet, because of all these changes. We as human beings are going to have to be ready, strong, centered and balanced to harmonize with events that will be happening in the future. The earth and the human race are coming to a peak in many areas, such as in population, the oil, economy, pollution, food shortage, religious and political issues.

27

People are carrying and dealing with more stress than ever before, because the world is becoming a smaller place due to communication and computers. The planet will be going through many natural global changes and shifts. Everyone will have to prepare himself and be aware and ready for the constant threat of terrorism acts throughout the world. There will be a continuous threat within this period of time. The only way to initially deal with this threat of terrorism is to first become totally secure and internally strong within yourself. This is a time on our planet in which we have to be incredibly strong mentally and become very flexible to bend with time and changes. As human beings, we now need to activate this warrior mentality. We must not only activate and develop it for ourselves, but for the benefit of all. Something will eventually have to give in all these areas, unless the pressure is released. We first must release the pressure and stress from within. The main deciding factors, which can really make a difference in the destiny of the human race, are our attitude and mentality. We must always attempt to see the bigger picture and not see only things with a linear segregated mentality. The more we perceive things from our own private interpretation, the more isolated our minds will become. We must attempt to see and perceive a problem, issue, or situation from all sides, before we make a decision. Everything in life can be taken away from us except one thing, our attitude. We will continually emphasize this statement throughout the book.

The more we can materialize the ideals of these warrior concepts in our daily lives, the more we can actually make a difference on our planet. The more you understand these warrior concepts, the more you will understand yourself, others, our planet and the universe. If you understand the essence of these warrior principles, you will better understand the major issues pressuring our earth and people today. This warrior mentality will give you the proper understanding, knowledge, concepts and principals to make the best and right decisions in life. We must continually practice to keep an open mind and a holistic mentality. These major elements will aid us in seeing things more clearly. We must first be able to look at ourselves clearly and strictly. We should criticize ourselves before we criticize others. In the samurai's code, they would say you have to be able to cut yourself before you cut others.

The warrior mentality is not concerned with just being stronger and more aggressive. It is a mentality of being more understanding and compassionate when appropriate. There is a time to fight and there is a time not to fight and harmonize. Fighting and doing battle is usually a last resort. If you don't fight, acquiring the warrior mentality will help you decide when it is appropriate to do battle. The warrior rarely draws his sword, but when he does, he makes a 100 percent commitment ... and it's to the death, if need be. If a small percentage of human beings continually make a commitment to push and better evolve themselves, this world will constantly be a better place.

What Is the Best State of Mind to Contemplate on the Warrior Concepts and Chapters?

It is much better to read or contemplate the warrior chapters and concepts when you are in a relaxed mental state. If you are not in that state, it is best to do some long relaxed breathing before you read. A stressed or hurried mind is a distracted mind. Attempt to relax your entire body from head to toe. Visualize and imagine any excess tension draining out of your body and every limb. This type of breathing will activate a calm alpha state of mind, conducive to reading, absorbing and reflecting. It is often referred to as a relaxed calm state of mind, which is better to absorb the contents and information. This basic type of breathing will help clear your mind. If you are a bit stressed or in a hurry, that will also affect the amount of information you will be able to absorb in the chapters. This type of breathing will also help to eliminate your stress.

It is also best to acquire open mind. You don't have to form an opinion on the material of each chapter, just keep an open mind.

Tom Muzila executing a side-thrust kick, during a SWAT Training Tactic seminar.

Let the information digest for a while. Contemplate the data, but try not to prejudge the information or content of each chapter. Let your mind soar, be free and liberated as you read. Remember the old saying, "Is your cup half filled or half empty?" Also, if your cup is already full, nothing else will fit in it. You would have to pour a certain amount of fluid out to fit a specific amount of knowledge or insight into it.

Remember again who you really are. You are a spiritual, magical being and soul in a physical body. Go back to believing in yourself again. You have the ability to focus on and create anything you would like with your mind and thoughts. Let go of any doubts you have held about yourself. It is difficult, because our minds are able to move so fast and soar—from the past to the present to the future—in a split second.

Most people have created many productive goals from their desires and attempted to reach them, but were unable to. Many people end up getting so let down that they don't care that much anymore and just give up in their attempt to achieve something. They just get through and survive that day. They let this happen in all facets of their life, career, relationships and personal growth. There are so many people that let this happen after years of getting disappointed and discouraged. Your mind eventually can get very discouraged, but you cannot let that happen. It is extremely hard to be up and positive in every moment, situation and scenario you experience.

You must also refrain from being too hard on yourself. You are not being defeated. You are making the conscious choice to decide to let yourself down. When something doesn't go the most positive way, many people start creating a pattern in their mind to get let down and defeated. Unfortunately, they end up supporting it, by saying, "I'll never be able to have or do that." As a result, they won't. You end up creating whatever you think about the most. If you continually dwell on and think about what you don't have and what you are lacking, your mind will continually create what you don't have. Go back to truly believing in yourself. Organize the patterns and priorities of your thoughts as you would in achieving any goal. Believe in the power of your thoughts, without any doubts, fears, insecurities and mental blocks. The more you are able to use, control and reorganize your thoughts, the more you will start noticing harmony in your life. Things will start going right for you. There will be many synchronicities that will start happening in your life, which just didn't happen by chance. Your life will start harmonizing with the people and situations going on all around you. You will get inspired, excited and motivated about truly living again. Even though you might not be able to directly change things around you at first, you can definitely change the way you think about them.

You have the abilities to create a dream life for yourself and everyone around you. Believe your life is special and magical and you will create it to be that way. Let's get started on that path to reorganize your thought patterns to create, accomplish and achieve any goal you desire.

Chapter 1

Facing Yourself

The concept of facing yourself has existed throughout human history in various cultures. It became very particularly pronounced, however, in the 13th century when Master Eisai (1146-1215) introduced Japan to Rinzai Zen. He opened a meditation hall at Kenninji in Kyoto. Eventually, his teachings started to spread through other provinces. Numerous samurai started integrating Eisai's teachings into their daily sword training routines. They found that they could better control their minds and in turn, raise the level of their sword fighting. Dogen (1200-1253) was the other Zen Patriarch who had a little variation in his teachings from that of Eisai. He started, what was called, Soto Zen. It was a little more liberal than Eisai's Rinzai Zen. There were many other sects of Zen starting at various monasteries in Japan, too. Zen is a specialized practice of a facet of Buddhism. These concepts made the spiritual, mental, technical and physical aspects of sword training evolve to its highest levels and over time became a major part of the samurai training and code. That code became known as Bushido, the way of the warrior. A Buddhist priest named Saicho, who lived 1200 years ago, remarked, "Even the dullest stone becomes sharp after 12 years of daily polishing." This statement became very popular in Tendai Buddhism.

These principles focused on completely controlling your

Tom Muzila on top of Mt. Shasta, after a fast challenging climb.

mind. If you could control your mind and use its higher potential, your sword practice and fighting would reflect your concentration. To acquire control of your mind, you first had to exist and
be totally in the present moment of your life. Nothing else existed except this moment. This became known as mindfulness or
using your mind to the fullest in that present moment. By being
in the moment, your mind wouldn't be distracted and attached
to something in the past. If you were fully in the moment, at your
best capacity, that positive moment would create the best future
moment or destiny for you. Your mind then wouldn't be distracted or thinking about the future. If these basic concepts were
adhered to, you could better yourself to the fullest capacity in
that present moment.

It became evident to better control one's mind one had to
face himself very strictly in every part of life. He could not let past
conditioned fears, insecurities and mental blocks control him or
he couldn't perform at his fullest capacity. What it all came down

to was a warrior's strongest, toughest opponent was himself. He must face himself strictly against all of his fears, insecurities, weakness, mental blocks and negative mental issues. The worst thing to do was to make excuses for these problems and run away from them, because they would get worse. The only option for a warrior was to face each one of them strictly and attempt to extinguish them from his consciousness. A warrior would make a practice of going out and doing what he feared most in life. It was discovered that the majority of fears were created in one's mind, through worries, desires and concerns for the future. A more recent and popular saying to define this process is taken from the acronym FEAR, false evidence appearing real. Basically, most people spend 85 percent of the time worrying and being too concerned about things that never actually happen. This is a major waste of mental energy and it only supports the negative conditioning of past mental patterns, which turn into daily habits and are exhibited in the activities of our daily lives and thinking.

The worse fear for samurai or warriors to face was death. A true samurai would make his daily practice in facing death. He felt if he could first face death and accept it, without being attached to it, all other major fears would also become eliminated from his life. The samurai and the true warrior gave as much importance to how they would face death as to how they would live. They would meditate on their death daily, not out of fear, but trying better to accept it. A warrior might think about all of the ways he could die in battle daily, such as sword cuts, spears, arrows, getting blown up, burned or committing hara-kiri (belly disembowelment). They would continually meditate and think about these types of deaths until they eventually accepted all of them. After they accepted them, they would not become fearful of or attached to any of them. If a true samurai faced a technical situation on the battlefield in which a decision would bring him life or death, the samurai would always pick death. If the warrior survived, he could live more mentally free and liberated and not be attached to that. He would have surpassed any mental limits he previously acquired. These elements of fearlessness and mental liberation would eliminate any limits on their thinking and they could raise themselves to unlimited mental and technical levels in swordsmanship on the battlefield. The samurai and warriors who trained this way would more easily accept their destiny in life and death.

The main technical aspect for a samurai to directly face himself was a practice called, "irimi"or "Gates of Heaven." Translated, this means entering technique or entering mentality. It is also referred to as, "getting into your opponent." In the arena of sword fighting, it is expressed in this statement, "Under the sword is hell and beyond the sword is heaven." We will discuss this more in a later chapter. "Irimi" is basically attacking your opponent straight in at the same moment he decides to attack you. If you have no mental blocks or fears and your attack is timed properly, you end up beating your opponent to the attack. A high level samurai would have to do this with a razor sharp sword. If he held back a split second, didn't have the right mentality, spirit and feared dying, he would surely die or be fatally injured. In karate, it's not as dangerous, as it would be using a live sword blade. You would put your face directly into your opponent's fist, with your hips directly in and under you. Again, with the right mentality, spirit and timing, your opponent's fist would graze your face at the same moment you would destroy him with your attack.

Harigaya Sekiun formally originated this practice with the sword in the 1500 to 1600 century in Japan. He had a habit of dulling his sword blade before he had a duel. He didn't want his sword blade to cut and get stuck in his opponent's sharp sword. Senior Okuyama, one of Tsutomu Ohshima's seniors, is said to have introduced and made this concept popular in karate in the early 1900s. Tsutomu Ohshima has kept this practice alive today in karate. He has made an intensive study of the results of teaching this "Gates of Heaven" concept for the last 50 years. He has found that if a student couldn't accomplish a certain degree of success in this practice, it was much easier for him to be swayed or distracted from being very straight and honest with himself the rest of his life. It was also noted that unique members, who had accomplished a high level of success of this "Gates of Heaven" practice, became high level martial artists or extremely successful individuals in their fields and professions. Ohshima discovered that a practitioner has to pass his or her mind through this gate legitimately. He cannot fake or modify the path. He has to face himself strictly. That is the only way he can authentically achieve some-

Tom Muzila throwing a 90-pound boulder in Switzerland. This is a popular event in the Alps.

thing very positive from this practice. Being successful at this one practice can and will affect the way a person faces his or her entire life.

Every major religion and serious spiritual path has its own type of Special Training, in which individuals and monks had the opportunity to push and face themselves beyond mental limits. Tibetan Buddhism started to become popular during the 13th century in Tibet. The first Dalai Lama was Gedun Truppa (1391-1474). He founded the Zhaxilhunbo Monastery and became its first abbot. He wrote several books, which included the Commentary to the Sutra of Commandment, Commentary on Logic and the Collection of Primary and Secondary Causes. He

Tom Muzila going down white water rapids with a friend in Idaho.

made many of his own contributions to Buddhist theory. These theories expanded through the Dalai Lamas that followed him to many types of Sutras, practicing doctrines and teachings. In Tibet, Mahayana Buddhism gave birth to Tantrism. This is also called Vajrayana (Diamond Way). Its precepts and principles were disciplined and a monk had to face himself strictly on every level and in every situation. That is why it was called, Diamond Way or Wisdom. The monks had to continually face any mental negativity they had and purify themselves mentally, physical and spiritually. Vajrayana also emphasized the teaching, "All is mind alone."

Our minds have an incredible capacity to expand, explore and evolve. The only limits we have on our consciousness are the ones we impose upon ourselves. Tsutomu Ohshima, my karate teacher was the first one to bring karate to America as an organization in 1955. He has constantly reminded his students, "Face Yourself." He always emphasized to us years ago that our fears, weaknesses, insecurities and mental blocks would materialize in a very strong, intense karate practice. As these negative elements arose, it was the practitioner's personal responsibility to face himself, strictly and honestly—throughout his training. If the individual were faced with a weakness and insecurity, he would face it and push himself harder through it. This would prove to his mind that it wasn't that big a deal in the first place. When an individual had some basic experience in facing himself, he would eventually integrate this philosophy into his daily life. If the individual were extremely honest with himself, this practice would spread over to his job, profession, and even relationships. The individuals who were able to bring this practice into their lives would be able to live their lives to a much fuller capacity. This element of facing yourself was very similar to that of the samurai. Even though it is an ancient concept it is still valid to us in contemporary society. We can still use this philosophy to better polish our minds and ourselves and become fuller and stronger human beings.

Chapter 2

A Warrior Never Gives Up

There is one unbeatable mark or goal. It is the, "I cannot do it" record. A true warrior never gives up. If someone says he cannot do something, he usually does not want to do it. Everyone has the capacity to accomplish whatever he really wants. He may also consider altering his strategy or attack plan. If you really want to accomplish something, you never give up. There are numerous stories throughout history of individuals who had goals, kept falling short, but eventually accomplished them. Thomas Edison failed in 17,000 experiments before he finally succeeded with the light bulb. Babe Ruth hit 714 home runs, but he also had 1,330 strikeouts. Albert Einstein was four before he could speak and seven before he could read. Isaac Newton did very poorly in his grad school. Walt Disney was fired, because his employer felt he wasn't creative enough. Hayden, who was Beethoven's teacher, gave up on him, because he felt he was a slow learner.

One of a warrior's main strengths is perseverance. He must be able to outlast everyone else. This could be in a fight, a battle, striving to reach a goal or to be successful, trying to sell a product or getting a business off the ground. A warrior normally tries to end a fight quickly, but he also has to train and prepare himself for the long haul. Most individuals are not prepared to train for the long run mentally and physically. You can train to

*Bruce Kanegai standing on top of a mountain, while running
the 220-mile John Muir Trail run in the High Sierras.*

hold out after everyone quits, you will be the victor just on that.
When a warrior trains and practices his art, he has to acquire an
unlimited mentality. He has to program his mind, so he can continue for indefinitely. This is why one of the toughest things for a
martial artist or athlete is to push himself in his training until he
actually passes out. Of course, it isn't good to do this if someone
isn't in good health or is simply too old. Our minds can be much
stronger than our bodies, we can push ourselves beyond these
limits we mentally place on ourselves and we can do this by sheer
will. When we are exhausted, our body will try to make any
excuse to our mind to stop or hold back. Mentally, we have the
power and will to ignore these excuses, ignore the pain and push
way beyond them. When we are able to push ourselves to this
degree, we get to experience a new dimension and capacity in
our mind, which we can transfer over to the rest of our lives.

A warrior has to keep in mind that when one door closes

another usually opens, and that will help him accomplish what he set out to do. He must keep his mind open to other options, possibilities and alternate ways to accomplish his goals. If an individual confronts a block wall in his goals or training, there is always a way to work around it. It's also important to remember that the tide always changes. If you persevere long enough the tide will eventually change in your favor. You just have to be mentally open and aware of the opportunity when it comes.

Bruce Kanegai running through the snow on his 220 mile John Muir Trail run in 1980.

Key Points

- The one unbeaten, untied mark is, "The I cannot" record.
- Persevere and never give up.
- When fate closes one door, it always opens up another.
- The tide always changes and will eventually change in your favor.
- Sometimes it's better to take a chance at something and miss than to have never tried.
- Remember the popular saying, "If you shoot at the moon and miss, you still may hit a star."

Chapter 3

The Secrets of Firewalking

Why do we have a chapter on the secrets of firewalking in a book about warrior principles? Because the mental elements required to accomplish a true firewalk are very similar to what a warrior has to face when he encounters his deepest mental blocks. On a minor mental level, it is also very similar to what a warrior has to go through before he goes into battle or prepares himself for a fight. It is very relative. When a warrior goes into a fight or battle, he doesn't know what to expect, nor does he know what is going to happen. He has to surrender to his abilities, strong mentality and to fate. It is similar when an individual decides to attempt to walk on red-hot wood coals. He believes he can do it, but there is an unknown factor of what is going to happen when he puts his foot on those coals. He has to surrender to his mental strength and fate. It is also very similar to making the decision to jump into a big black hole. You don't know if the black hole is three feet or 100 feet deep. You have to depend on your mental strength and fate, which will get you through without being killed. You can see that the mental process you take yourself through to get ready to walk on red-hot coals is very similar to the mental process you take yourself through before you engage in a fight or battle. There are many skeptics who claim firewalking is not a big feat and almost anyone can do it. I agree, almost anyone can do it, if he or she really believes they

An individual preparing the red hot coals,
prior to Tom Muzila walking on them.

can do it. It is not that big a feat. But, most people believe they cannot do it and wouldn't even think about doing it, much less even attempt it. They fail, before they even consider the possibilities. Why? Because for their whole life they have been mentally programmed that fire will burn. Yes it will, but that too is relative to time, physical matter and intensity. If a person is going to successfully execute a firewalk, he first has to totally believe that he can do it. He must believe he can jump into this unknown dimension and survive, unharmed.

I performed firewalks for more than 10 years quite consistently. I walked over that 12- to 15-foot pit of red-hot glowing coals more than 100 times. I saw many people refuse to do it. If they had opened their mind and believed they could do it, they could have; I knew they could. I also saw a few people get burned and acquire some sizable blisters. I also got burned a couple of times and received some pretty good blisters. The times I got burned I noticed that I wasn't in the proper mentality to do the firewalk. You have to get yourself in a very meditative state, similar to the mental state you get yourself into before you fight in karate. Eric Best is the man who trained me to do firewalks. He was a scientist who never practiced the martial arts, but he had a very good understanding of basic martial art mental principles. He was also an excellent firewalk teacher.

To execute a firewalk, you have to believe completely that you can do it. Just like you have to totally believe you can go into battle or a fight. You may have to counter all of your habitual belief patterns. Your mind will possibly make you feel fear and think of negative things that could possibly happen. Your mind can be incredibly creative to find all of the possible excuses why you shouldn't be doing this. It will use scientific facts, logic, reason and basic common sense. You will have to fight every element, as it comes up in your mind with your mental strength and willpower. Basically, you must be able to accept every negative thing that can happen to you, from minor to major. You must also be able to accept every possible positive element you will acquire and how it will benefit you by accomplishing this feat. You cannot be mentally attached to either one. You must also accept the same possible positive and negative benefits of going into battle. This is very important; our beliefs can protect us or destroy us in firewalking, martial arts, karate or battle. It all depends on how we use them.

So, what mental process do you go through to accomplish a successful firewalk? You must first eliminate all of your fears about doing the firewalk. You must accept the negative and the positive elements that can happen and not be mentally attached to them. Sometimes it is good to make an attempt to bond with the fire and become one mentally with it. It is not your enemy; it is an ally. You can do this by meditating in front of the fire, while you are burning down the coals. Write down all of your negative fears, insecurities and mental blocks on paper and throw them in the fire. Then, write down all of the positive elements you can acquire from doing the firewalk and throw that paper in the fire.

If you want to experience the optimum benefits of accomplishing a firewalk, it is better to do it for purely internal mental elements. I recommend you don't execute it for any of the following three reasons:

- Don't do it to compete with anyone else.
- Don't do it to prove yourself.
- Don't do it for egotistical reasons.

When you are able to believe, you can accomplish the firewalk mentally. You have to get yourself in a very focused, concentrated, powerful mental state. You must keep your breathing in your lower abdomen, exhale longer and deeper. Hold your breath back slightly in the back of your throat, keep your mouth closed and exhale through your nose. Imagine that you are walking on cool green grass or moss and not red-hot coals. Don't imagine you are walking on ice. Your subconscious mind will not believe it or accept it. Do not look at the red-hot coals. Look slightly up, at an angle and out, with a very extensive projecting feeling. When you look up slightly, it helps project your mind out of your body. If you look down, it connects your mind with your emotional feelings, which you do not want to do for the firewalk. Start your walk with that type of feeling and mentality. Keep your mind empty, without any thoughts. If you think anything, think cool moss, cool moss, cool moss. Do not change your mentality until you are well off of the coals. It is very easy to physically do a firewalk. The hardest part is to believe you can, to have and hold the proper mentality and keep your faith in your higher consciousness or self. This is a similar mentality the warrior has to acquire before he fights or goes into battle.

Key Points

- WARNING! Do not attempt to accomplish a firewalk without a veteran expert specialist firewalk instructor.
- Believe with all of your being that you can accomplish this and counter all your habitual belief patterns.
- Accept all the negative things that can happen to you while doing this.
- Accept all of the positive elements that can benefit you from accomplishing this.
- Understand how your belief principles can protect you or destroy you in a firewalk, fight, battle or life.
- Be able to mentally jump into the black hole, whether it is three or 100 feet deep.
- Surrender your fate to your higher consciousness and mentality.

Chapter 4

Eliminate Fears
in the Martial Arts

Y ou will be able to utilize these same concepts and process-
es to help eliminate fears in any type of activity, sport or
business, you are active in, even though the theme is martial arts. The process is the same and the subject is relative. Our
biggest enemy in life is not the external situation we face; instead,
it is our internal and mental make-up, which gives us our perception of the world around us. It is not what happens to us that
determines the quality of our life. It is what we do with it that
makes the difference. As human beings, our three worst enemies
in life are fear, guilt and ignorance. The main one we're going to
deal with here is fear, but you would deal with the others in a very
similar manner.

As mentioned earlier, the best acronym I've ever heard for
the word FEAR is: false evidence appearing real. We say false,
because your mind may make up all of the horror stories to bring
on fear, but the action hasn't happened yet and it may not.
Remember, as human beings, generally we worry about 75 to 85
percent of the time about concerns that never happen. In reality,
it would be more realistic to be concerned about the 15 to 25
percent which does happen. On the other end of the scale, even

Tom Muzila working with one of Roland Duval's attack dogs in Ottawa, Canada.

if the negative action does happen to you and does hurt or kill you, your mind still has the capacity of not feeling fear. Our mind has tremendous abilities, and we have the choice of being in control of it or not.

There are many things a martial artist can fear throughout the years of his practice. It is the same for us as human beings. We have and acquire many fears throughout our lifetime. We have many fears of things that never happen to us. We also acquire fears, because of situations or experiences we have. We label and file them as positive or negative. The most important element is our perception and belief system. We filter certain experiences through the foundation of our perception and belief system and that determines how we will interpret an experience we have in martial arts or life. Our minds will create a fear and mental block or a positive realization, from which we can learn. It all depends on our perception and how we are wired up mentally. The emotion of fear is so relative. Every person's perception of fear is different. This is also why in court, regarding a self-defense situation, the accused is always advised to say, "I feared for my life." This escalates the threat to a potential life-or-death scenario. That gives the defendant accused more flexibility in defending himself.

A martial artist can have fear of getting hit. Fear of the pain the muscles feel from staying in low stances. He can be fearful of tougher and stronger opponents. He may have fears of not practicing, fighting or performing well. The main fear, which many people have, is of not being able to push themselves beyond all mental and physical limits. When the mind pushes the body beyond unlimited capacities, the mind can create any excuse possible not to have to push itself to this intensity. Many fears will come up in a person's mind when he attempts to push himself beyond any mental and physical limitations. Basically, everyone creates the reality of fears in martial arts or life in their mind. The object is to continue to push through them, and the mind realizes that it is not so bad or even painful and it can be done.

Tsutomu Ohshima occasionally brings up another old saying. "If you don't want to get wet, jump in the lake!" If you stand on the edge and anticipate how cold the water will be or just put your foot in and attempt to get warmed up to make it easier to get in, it will make it worse. If you just jump in all at once, you will feel the cold for a moment, but you will quickly realize that it's not bad as you anticipated. This is usually the best way to face most fears. Face them straight and head on. Don't make excuses or run away from them, because they will always follow you. You can also take the fear and face it in very small steps; this will help build your confidence to face it on a larger scale. Never try to analyze the fear when you are in a fearful state of mind. Your solutions will always be warped if you are not in a clear, calm objective mind when you attempt to analyze your fears.

If you really want to help eliminate your fears, you first have to recognize that you have a fear. You have to determine specifically what the fear is. Then it is good to calculate exactly what caused or created the fear and determine from where it came. You should then analyze what benefit the fear has been to you until now. How has having the fear kept you from getting hurt or possibly injured, mentally, emotionally or physically? Now analyze why it is beneficial to be free of the fear and how that will benefit your training, practice, yourself and your life. If you first think about the fear in this manner, it will really help you to decide whether you really have the will, desire and passion to get rid of it. Then, when you decide you are ready, no matter what you have to go through to get rid of the fear, you will do it. Now you are truly ready.

Again the steps: Identify the fear or say hello to it. Analyze the fear from every angle and point of view. See it from all angles objectively. Then be willing to accept the worse that can happen to you, by facing it. Also, be willing to accept all of the positive elements that will happen to you by eliminating the fear. Then take action on your fear, by taking the first step to face it.

Let's look at fear like an object. First, some people come up to the fear and realize it makes them feel very uncomfortable. They immediately run away from it. Others will totally ignore the fear and not even recognize it. They won't deal with it at all. Still others feel the fear. They will have the vibrant sense of fear, but they will just sit and wade in those feelings and feel sorry for themselves. They will make excuses for themselves, become a victim and try to make other people feel sorry for them. And there are these, who will aggressively attack the fear and make it look like they are being brave and facing the fear, but it is only on the surface. It is only an external show for other people and these types of people end up still dragging the fear along with them and are still attached to the fear. The best way to face a fear is to recognize it, go up to it, feel it a bit, maybe sit in it for awhile, but make sure you experience it from a very objective level. Do not experience it from an emotional or reactive mental state. Study and feel the fear calmly and objectively, then pass through it so your mind can understand it is not so bad.

Key Points
- FEAR is "false evidence appearing real."
- If you don't want to get wet, jump in the lake.
- Recognize you have a fear. Identify it. What is it?
- Analyze the fear. What caused it?
- Ask yourself how, has it benefited you until now.

Tom Muzila executing a parachute jump in the late 1980's. He has jumped numerous times and continually attempts to face himself on many levels.

- Be willing to accept the worse things that can happen to you by facing the fear.
- Why be free of the fear?
- Be willing to accept the best and most positive things that can happen to you by eliminating the fear.
- Take action. Face and eliminate your fear.
- Start with basic or simple steps until you have the ability and self-confidence to face and work the bigger ones.

Chapter 5
Special Training

There have been numerous warriors and top-caliber athletes throughout history who had the mentality and consciousness to be able to push themselves beyond any mental and physical limitations. To be in total control of their mind and body, they pushed themselves through an enormous amount of pain and exhaustion. They did this for many reasons, but the most important one was so they could perform much better in battle, or excel at the top of their sport or art. They faced all their fears, mental blocks and attachments, as they didn't want to be hindered by them in battle. By doing this, these top warriors became mentally free and liberated in their thinking.

The ability to push oneself to maximum extremes is not only practiced by the top warriors. Numerous people in all types of arts, sports and activities practice this essence, wanting to achieve the highest level they can in their art. It doesn't matter whether one is a painter, artist, mountain climber, musician or athlete. An individual has to be able to push himself strictly to mentally pass through this level. When an individual is finally able to push himself beyond all limits with the appropriate mentality, a whole new world will be opened up to him.

The Japanese samurai were one of the earliest cultures to make an art of pushing themselves through their rigorous training. As mentioned in Chapter One, Zen was introduced to Japan in the early 1200s. When some of the top samurai started practicing Zen, they found the level of their mental and technical swordsmanship really excelled. By practicing these various mental concepts in Zen, these samurai found they could push themselves beyond any limits. There are records of two yamabushi (mountain monks) who participated in a 50-day Special Training. It was noted that they executed 113,880 sword combination techniques in this 50-day period. It was not recorded how many hours these practitioners trained everyday. A modern day sword expert studied these techniques and excelled at them. He practiced them until he felt it was humanly impossible to execute them at a faster and more realistic pace. He calculated that these two warrior monks had to have trained 22 hours a day to execute that many techniques in 50 days. This was one of the earliest recorded Special Trainings.

In the 1850s, a top samurai came along, later considered the last of the greatest samurai. His name was Tesshu Yamoaka. The swordsmanship school he attended had a three-, five- and seven-day Special Training. It would take a practitioner about three years of consistent, intense training to prepare for any of these Special Training sessions. These training sessions would require a student to get up very early in the morning and practice intensely for about 12 hours straight. Using a wooden bokken, a senior would line up in front of the student and continuously spar with him. Then the next senior would take over, again and again for the entire day. The student could not rest; only the seniors would take turns and be able to rest. When Tesshu Yamoaka went through this he made three, five, seven and 10 days of this type of Special Training. He didn't stop because he couldn't continue; he stopped because all of his seniors couldn't continue. That is an example of how mentally strong he became.

There is another exceptional spiritual, mental, physical practice and philosophy that has been going on in Japan for a thousand years. This practice is its own unique Special Training. It is a part of Tendai Buddhism, which also includes meditation, pre-

Special Training in Japan, in the 1960's. Tsutomu Ohshima (3rd from left, front row). Senior Toshio Kamata-Watanabe (4th from left, front row).

cepts, esotericism, nature worship and practice for salvation of sentient beings. It is called kaihogyo or the "mountain marathon," which exceptional monks participate in on Mount Hiei. Most of the monks undergo an intensive training, just to be accepted and approved to participate in the kaihogyo. These monks are called the marathon monks of Mount Hiei, also the white cranes of Hiei. They still go through this mountain pilgrimage today. John Stevens wrote a book about them with the same name in the late 1980s. Basically, the monks run and jog 18 to 30 miles everyday and even up to 52 1/2 miles a day in the later portion of the practice phase. The complete phase of training lasts for seven years or 1,000 days. They are running a marathon, almost every single day for seven years. After seven years of, they have run the equivalent of circling the equator or the distance of 1,000 marathons. During the runs, they have to hit 255 stations of worship everyday, which are all types of spiritual scenes, statues and sacred spots. The routes take them through dense forests, up

A Summer Special Training in the mid-1980's, around the Santa Barbara, California area. The group is executing 100 intense (Tekki-katas), in a practice. There are about 250 people in attendance.

around mountains, over thousands of stairs, mountain streams, inclines, declines and through parts of cities. In the winter, the monks continue the marathon in freezing temperatures in the snow. These monks don't wear Nikes or even jogging shoes; they wear traditional straw sandals. Sometimes they go through three to five sandals a day. During the entire day route, path and course, the monks only sit for a few minutes one time. They do this to do a short chant (mantra) or prayer. They exist on a minimal amount of vegetables, rice, soups and liquids. Their diet is equivalent to only about 1,450 calories a day. Any other professional athlete could never survive on the small amounts that these monks exist on. On the 750th day, the monks go through a practice called doiri, which continues for nine days on average. In these nine days, they fast no food, no water and no sleep. A few hundred years ago they would do doiri for 10 days, but many of the monks would die. In recent times, they lowered it to seven and one-half from nine days. Most monks stated that the hardest and most grueling element of this practice was to try to keep their head erect along with not being able to rest the entire time. After years of practice, a monk who becomes an expert can rest for ten minutes, and this is equal to five hours of normal sleep. The monks would really try to face themselves and face death and accept it everyday of the training. They would face each day like it was their last on earth. This intense training was lengthened to 21 years in the Kamakura period. The first seven years was under a scholar monk and focused on fundamental study topics. The second seven years concentrated on the Tendai Doctrine. The last seven years stressed personal contemplation.

There have only been 46 monks who accomplished the 1,000-day marathon between 1885 and 1988. Few people are drawn to this, much less able to complete these superhuman feats. Out of these, there were two monks who completed two full seven-year terms. One of them died on the 2,500 day of the practice. One exceptional monk completed three full seven-year terms. His name was Okuno Genjun. The average age of most of the marathon monks was about 30. The oldest monk, whose name was Sakai was 61 by the time he completed his 2,000-day marathon. There were numerous monks who died during the marathon mountain pilgrimage through the years. One of the mentally and spiritually strongest monks was a man named, Hakozaki. It was recorded that he accomplished the nine-day fast (doiri) without food, water, sleep and rest an amazing 36 times from 1948 to 1973.

Tsutomu Ohshima went through many karate Special Training during the early 1950s at Waseda University in Japan. In addition to seven-day Special Trainings that were held four times a year, they also had some 10-day sessions. He attended all of these. Many of the intense practices were well over three to five hours long. Some of these Special Trainings were held on an island, and there are stories of a student occasionally attempting to swim away from the island to the mainland to get out of the intense training sessions. In 1955, Tsutomu Ohshima brought

*The first group meditation, at the third 24-Hour Karate Practice,
led by Tom Muzila. It was held in 1986 in the high Sierra mountain's.
Fifty-five karate members attended.*

karate to America and started the first karate association. He held
the first karate Special Training here in America in 1959. There
were seven in attendance and all were either brown or white
belts. They were Caylor Adkins, George Marakami, Roe Suzuki,
Curtis Adkins, Jerry Emery, Don Ridgeway and James Cross. On
the first morning of the early training session, Mr. Ohshima wait-
ed downstairs for the members, but no one came down. He had
to go and energetically wake each person up. The Americans
were not used to this type of intense practice at first, but Mr.
Ohshima knew they had a huge potential. Mr. Ohshima based
this Special Training on ones he had done in Japan and Special
Training became what it is today.

Special Training is an important concept and it makes
Shotokan Karate of America and all of our other Shotokan groups
of the world unique from any other karate or martial arts group.
Special Training is the essence of our karate practice. This essence
cannot be found in words; it must be experienced. It is the fun-

damental element that exits throughout our entire karate practice. The benefits of Special Training ignite the rest of our techniques and tactics to be more effective in real combat. It is central to making our mind and body work as one unit. It is the glue that connects our practice to become one. It also connects our practice to become one with life.

Our three- and four-day intensive Special Training gives students, members and black belts an opportunity to be able to push themselves beyond any physical and mental limitations. They execute thousands of punches and kicks and hundreds of kata under incredibly intensive training conditions. They stand in a horse-stance for 90 minutes and have little rest and sleep. Special Training is the most important way a member can face and push him or herself strictly and raise his mental capacity. When members push themselves at Special Training, their mental blocks, weaknesses, insecurities, fears and phobias arise. They

Tom Muzila (lower left), leading the first straight through 24-Hour Karate Practice in the San Jacinto Mountains in 1975. Don Depree, Greg Scott and Randy McClure first row, left to right.

Tesshu Yamaoka, one of the last great sword masters, who lived in the mid-1800's. He passed away while meditating and his internal spirit and will still kept him sitting upright.

then have a chance to face that mental block, push through it and eliminate it. The more Special Training an individual attends, with the appropriate mentality to face himself, the more he will eliminate his mental blocks and help create a much stronger, limitless liberated mentality. This will not only help his karate mentality to evolve, but it will also raise his technical level. That stronger mentality can then spread over to his daily life and the way he perceives life. After attending numerous Special Trainings with a strict mentality, students naturally acquire a better individual philosophy to become more accomplished and successful in other spheres of their lives.

Through the years, I have seen many people push themselves to incredible degrees at our own three- and four-day Special Trainings. We have had Special Trainings in the winter when it was extremely cold. We have had them in the summer when it was hot. They have been in the rain, in the mountains or on the beach and in all types of climates, elevations and environments. I personally helped lead one, where we actually ran in the snow for awhile, and no one got frostbite. Every Special Training is very different and unique, even though we execute the same practices in all of them. It is the different individuals who push themselves beyond mental limits, the various atmospheres that aid to make each one slightly unique and different.

Sometimes big, powerful men really had some problems doing it. I've also seen individuals you would never suspect that could push and drive themselves beyond all limits, especially women. The hardest self-practice is to stand in a lower continuous horse stance for 90 minutes. This is a true test of the power of our minds. Many people automatically put a governor on their minds and will stay on this side of the edge. They will stay a specific height to be able to make it through with a certain amount of pain. Then there are the limited few who will stand extremely low for the whole time. They truly jump into the deep black hole, not knowing what to expect. They face a tremendous amount of pain and will possibly even pass out, but they acquire an incredible mental strength and are able to tap into that the rest of their lives. It is amazing to see the way certain people train before going to Special Training and then see the difference after they go. Many become a real tiger inside and are able to use that to change the way they approach and experience their life. Of course, this is just an example of what an intense karate Special Training can do when someone applies the appropriate mentality. Numerous other individuals have or create their own Special Trainings in life. Exceptional sports athletes push themselves all the time to break all limits and barriers. The capacity we have as human beings can be amazing. The most important element is to have and create the continuous experiences to be able to push yourself beyond all limits ... mentally, physically and spiritually.

Chapter 6

The Power of Belief

Belief is the most powerful mental attribute. The power of belief can sometimes accomplish miracles. We experience our whole lives through what our belief system is. We see our lives through what beliefs we have created. There is an old saying, "We see what we believe, not believe what we see!" We perceive things and experiences in life, because of what we believe. Nothing is life has meaning, except the meaning we give it. We give importance to certain things and experiences in life, because of what we believe. We create our reality and level of karate and martial arts through our belief principles in life. If we believe we are a great fighter and martial artist, we will find ways to make that happen. We will also put an emphasis on certain parts of training that we believe will make us a great fighter. We will become what we believe and see ourselves to be in our minds. We are the result of what we think and believe. Remember the saying, "Whatever you believe and conceive you can achieve."

If a person totally believes he is a great fighter and cannot be beaten, he can easily have the edge over a more technically skilled fighter with more experience. The more energy, emotion, commitment and importance you put behind your beliefs, the more power you will have. If someone completely decides not to give up or surrender under any conditions and holds that strong mental commitment, he is going to be extremely hard to beat. It

Tom Muzila executing an upper-level round kick, next to an F-16 Fighter Jet he was getting prepared to pull at Hills Airforce Base, Utah.

is much harder to fight a person, even if he doesn't have any fighting skills, if he decides you will have to kill him to beat him. There have been numerous stories of soldiers in battles who were not fatally wounded but still died from the wounds, because they believed they couldn't survive. There have also been many accounts of brave soldiers who were critically wounded but survived, because they willed themselves to survive. Not only can you control the amount of stress you can endure in training and in life, you also have the power to determine what experiences you will register as stressful and how stressful these situations really are.

Everything we do in karate, martial arts and life is done to create a certain mental and emotional state. We train and push ourselves to be able to acquire a certain accomplished confident state of mind. If we win a million dollars, it's not the million dollars that makes us happy. It is the mental state or the emotional liberation and freedom of having the million dollars that is most important. We have certain rules in our minds that have to be met to create a specific mental state. We link outside experiences or technical situations that have to be met to triggering a certain mental state. We also have the power to make those beliefs and rules in our minds a little easier, so those mental states can be achieved more easily. We can also make those beliefs and rules much harder to be met in our minds, so those positive mental states are more difficult to be met. We have the power in our belief systems to make things happen. We can create and accomplish any level we believe we can in martial arts and in life.

Everyone makes decisions based on his belief system. One small basic decision can radically change your life, which can make it go from plus to minus or minus to plus. How your belief system is wired is very important. The importance you put on your training and practice all depends on your belief system. These decisions are filtered through an individual's beliefs and values. Your decisions shape your life more than anything else. Generally, people do more to avoid pain rather than gain pleasure. Your beliefs determine whether you'll feel pain or pleasure from an experience. A true warrior will face the pain he feels during training and practice and will mentally push beyond it. He will not put that much importance on the pain he is feeling. It is just a feeling like other types of feelings. He labels and files it differently in his mind. There is no hard and easy for a warrior. Also, what he likes and dislikes doesn't exist. He just programs to do whatever it takes to accomplish something. Your values, based on your beliefs, are the direction your life and training will go.

There are two main categories of basic thought that determine the way we perceive things based on our beliefs. The first category is acceptance, open-mindedness, surrender and love. The second is doubt, fear, insecurity and mental blocks. The first area is a plus and generates an expanding mentality. The second area is considered more of a minus and contracts our mentality. Every action taken by a human being is based on the thought of an open mentality (expanding) or a fearful mentality (contracting). Our deepest inner voice or subconscious mind decides whether the thoughts are based on love or fear. An individual's belief must be intense enough, that his subconscious mind accepts it. A fearless warrior is always ready to face challenges and throw any doubts he has away, because he knows it will only hinder him. The warrior is ready to jump into the black hole.

Many years ago, I was reading some interesting esoteric information, which I was extremely concentrated and focused on. I was also heating up a pan of soup for lunch on the stove, which I let burn. I took the pan off the stove and put it on the table next to a cold glass of water, while still attempting to read the material. I slowly reached over to pick up the glass of water to get a drink. At the moment the tips of my fingers started to touch something, I remembered the red-hot pan was also there. For some reason, in my mind, I fully believed I touched the pan. When I felt my fingers touch something, with that intense belief in my mind, I felt the heat and the tip of my fingers getting burned. I even heard a slight hiss in my mind. I quickly jerked my hand away. I looked up and realized that I didn't touch the red-hot pan, but I had touched the ice-cold glass of water. I looked at my fingertips and they had little red spots on the tips. I also felt a slight burning sensation. I couldn't believe it. I had actually slightly burned the tips of three fingers on a moist glass of ice-cold water, because I believed so intensely that it was the red-hot pan.

So, how strong and powerful is belief? I heard a question was asked in a book pertaining to the power of belief. Someone asked, "If belief was that powerful, why can't we grow an arm or a leg?" Answer; "Because no-one believes that we can!" The book was, Ask and it is Given by Esther and Jerry Hicks.

Caylor Adkins and Sadaharu Honda demonstrating martial art resuscitation techniques during the first 5th-degree black belt (godan) ranking test in 1976.

Key Points

- Eliminate any doubts you have from your consciousness.
- Believe in yourself.
- Believe in your tactics, techniques and abilities.
- Build your belief system from a bigger perspective of life.
- Create your belief system so it will be easier for you to be successful.
- Balance your belief system, so it will not be contrary to your training or life.

Chapter 7

Mental Conditioning and Non-attachment

Mental conditioning and non-attachment are actually two opposite conditions. Each one can be positive or negative, depending on the degree of how strongly mentally conditioned we are and how mentally non-attached we are to certain things and experiences in life. We must have a balance between both. For example, if we are too conditioned to react a specific way to an experience in life, we will not be open to understanding it from any other perspective. This will make us extremely biased on a particular issue. On the other hand, if we train our minds to respond in a positive way in an emergency situation or in an unavoidable situation to, that conditioning is positive.

What about non-attachment? If we feel bad, upset or even guilty about a certain situation that is not our fault, we are placing ourselves under considerable stress. However, the situation was not our fault, and we should not blame ourselves or hold ourselves responsible. We should mentally let it go and not be attached to it, so it will not bother us consciously or subconsciously. By contrast, suppose we did something that hurt someone else, didn't take responsibility for our actions and just let it go mentally. That would be considered morally irresponsible, even though we were not

Frank Lopes, (facing, far right) a war veteran, still became one of Tsutomu Ohshima's top fighters, even though he was critically wounded in the Korean War.

attached to the thoughts or situation. The distinction here of course is between what is and is not within our control. You can see there are positives and negatives to each state. The ability to condition our minds with positive elements and also be non-attached where appropriate can really benefit our mentality and understanding.

People get attached and mentally conditioned to many things in life. The most common attachments are training, jobs, professions, beliefs, principles, relationships, abilities and habits. An extreme attachment either way is negative. You have to train your mind to still be very open to other points of view and understandings. These habits will also help your karate or martial arts training. Consider the ways people shape their lives by their beliefs and philosophies. These can direct the whole destiny of theirs lives and how they will perceive every experience they have. Let's take an even smaller distinction, hard and easy. Most people usually pick the easier way of doing and getting things. That may be good for some things, but not for others. A true warrior who is on the path usually always picks the harder way, and this builds stronger character and inner willpower. Or consider someone always conditioned to doing what he likes without thinking of long-run consequences for himself or others. This one element will completely rule his whole life. Many times, to learn and grow in life, we will have to do things that we don't like at all, but these experiences will develop and help us to evolve to a much higher mentality. So basically, the best mentality is not to be attached to doing things and having experiences in life because they are hard or easy or because you like or dislike them. You attempt to become non-attached to those elements and do them, because they will help you grow and evolve mentally. You have to keep looking at the bigger picture in life. Sometimes you have to make yourself do things which you normally wouldn't in order to grow.

The mind is like a plant. It only grows as big as the pot you plant it in. Some scientists did an experiment with a mackerel and a barracuda in the same aquarium wherein a piece of glass divided the tank and separated the fish. The barracuda kept trying to get to the mackerel. Every time he did, however, he bumped his nose on the glass. He eventually became conditioned to think he couldn't go over there. The scientist then removed the glass and the barracuda still didn't cross over into the other side of the tank. Here is a statement, which depicts non-mental attachment is an eastern religion. Buddhism, has the well-known line, "If you see the Buddha on the road, kill him." That doesn't mean to actually kill him. What it does mean is that you should not be mentally attached and conditioned to depend on him. Instead, you should depend on yourself. A warrior always depends on himself. Similarly, imagine you are on a hiking trip and you come to a river. You have a canoe with you. You use the canoe to cross the river, but when you start to go up over the mountains, you don't take the canoe with you. You do the same thing in your mind. Use thoughts that are to your advantage and then let them go. Don't be attached mentally to them.

There is an old story, which took place a few hundred years ago in Japan. The lord of a province in Japan was an expert swordsman. He received a letter from an individual asking him, "What is the essence of swordsmanship?" The lord felt he wasn't worthy to answer the question, so he decided to send the letter to his master, the notable Zen master Takuan. Master Takuan said that when you face an opponent, you don't get too focused or attached to his sword, hands or feet; otherwise, your mind will become imprisoned to one of those elements and you will not be able to see anything else. If you get too attached to who the swordsman is or how many men he has killed, your mind will become too imprisoned with those thoughts and you will not be able to move freely. Takuan also said that a better element to focus on is your breathing in your lower abdomen and direct your energy out through your opponent. Your mind will not be attached to any particular thing and you can express yourself more freely.

If you really want to change a negative habit, you must be willing to commit a radical positive act to change and show yourself that you are serious about the decision and, commitment to change. You must train yourself to interrupt negative patterns instantly to break old habits. For example, when you are having a conversation and someone interrupts, you forget what you were talking about when you resume talking. In this case, you should create a powerful, pleasant alternative pattern to eventually take its place. You have to constantly keep breaking the pattern every chance you get. It is extremely hard to just stop something cold. You must replace it with something else positive to refocus that

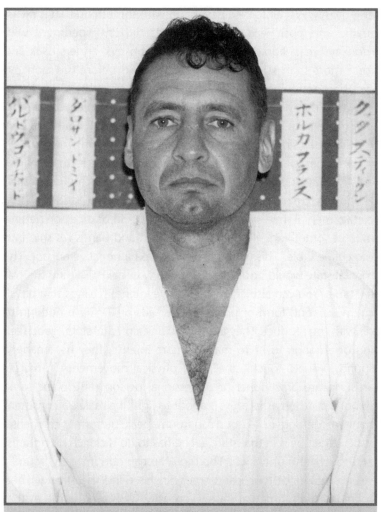

Jordon Roth was one of Tsutomu Ohshima's original six black belts in the United States.
The Japanese karateka named
him Tettsui-san, *which means hammer fists, after they saw him fight in Japan in 1967.*

energy. Always reinforce a new habit with something that is pleasurable and positive for you. Scientists did an experiment with monkeys years ago. They moved the monkeys' fingers back and forth more than 10,000 times. It took weeks before the monkeys did the same thing on their own. Then the scientists did it again, but this time they associated something pleasurable with the finger movement. The monkeys took less than 24 hours to start moving their fingers on their own with the same movement.

Another popular mental conditioning concept that martial artists, karate-ka, fighters and even business people can use is called anchoring; creating an association between a specific trigger and a certain mental state. A negative example would be a person getting mad at something. He then turns around and bangs his shin into the coffee table. This would be considered a negative anchor. The mental state would be anger associated with pain of hitting the coffee table. You can also link very positive intense feelings to a physical movement, form or posture. Most ads on TV have nothing to do with the product. They attempt to link a mental state, good feeling or emotion to it. To make it more intense, they use imagery, sounds, visuals, touch, smell, and physical movements. A martial artist, karate practitioner or professional person can do the same thing. Before a martial artist is about to fight, he makes a consistent habit of getting in a good optimum peak performance mental state. When he is in that state, all he has to do is clench his right fist and touch his right thigh. The more he can add imagery, sounds, visuals, senses of touch and smells in his mind the stronger and more intense his mental state. Eventually, whenever he makes that fist and touches his thigh that movement will automatically start creating and triggering his peak performance mental state.

Key Points

- Condition your mind to respond positively to survival or fighting situations.
- Train your mind to become non-attached to thoughts or situations that could be negative to your life. Let them go.
- Always replace negative habit patterns with positive patterns.
- Those new positive patterns, which will become your new habits, should be associated with something pleasurable or positive in your life or training.
- Practice anchoring techniques to trigger optimum peak performance mental states.
- Don't be worried or too concerned about the future.
- Don't waste your life on regrets.
- Nothing remains in the mind.
- Continually adjust your mind to reality.
- We are overwhelmed with information but starving for wisdom.

Chapter 8

Controlling Thoughts

It is amazing how powerful thoughts are. Most people don't realize the strong affect that their thoughts and thinking habits have upon their lives. Thoughts are the most powerful force in the universe. Your thoughts manifest your reality. You will become the type of person that you picture and think about most in your mind. The Buddha said, "We are the result of what we think." We have 60,000 to 90,000 thousand thoughts a day. Some people have more and others less. If 30,000 of those thoughts are negative or doubtful, that is one-third to on-half the total. Those negative thoughts program your mind to think in negative patterns. This can relate to how you solve problems, deal with important decisions in life and many other things. In one hour, 58 percent of our thoughts are focused either, on the past or the future and not on the present. Many of these thoughts are focused on worries or concerns that never even happen. You can see what a waste of energy this can be and how this can affect your training, business, relationships and life. Can you imagine if you put 100 percent of your thoughts and energy into the present moment, an important decision or solving a problem the proper way? You would solve the problem much faster, in the best and most appropriate way, which would be the best for you and everyone else. This can also be referred to as being mindful, using a much bigger capacity of your mentality.

The most important person you can have a good conversation with is yourself. If you talk down to yourself continuously, you will a create negative pattern and lower your self-confidence. Everyone executes mind talk. Everyone talks to himself. You must talk to yourself in a positive manner and with self-confidence, if you want to create positive thought patterns that will benefit you.

Emotion is energy in motion. Thoughts are pure energy. There is a theory that claims the energy of thoughts never dies. Those thoughts go out in the universe and attract like thoughts. Like attracts like, positive or negative. What you think expands, like the universe. If you think plus, it expands. If you think minus, it expands. If you think about what you don't have too much of, then what you don't have expands, too. The mind will attract to you what you think about most. Sometimes you can attract what you fear most. This is why some people who have a terrible fear of drowning, falling or being burned end up dying that way. That fear occupied a major portion of their thoughts and eventually created a pattern and attracted the actual event to them that they feared.

We have a real miracle continuously happening with our thoughts. Light and its essential character is that organism through which thought moves, works and has its being. Light is incandescent at a certain rate of vibration. It can also be as opaque and hard as steel at other tones and wavelengths. Light is still a great mystery to mortal individuals. The understanding of light is still believed by many scientists and masters to contain the secret of finite universe and matter. Nikola Tesla was a renowned electrical engineer and inventor, who lived in the early 1900s. He devoted his whole life to studying and experimenting with the essence of light and electromagnetic fields. He was experimenting to find out whether we could use light and electromagnetic fields to create and tap into natural energies. Take the essence of a tree, as an example. The tree takes the form of light in the ether, before it takes that pattern in reality. The light form is there and the pattern molecules respond to it. The pattern molecules are the protons and electrons in a given amount, which will formulate the tree. In Tendai Buddhism, monks believe even trees, bushes, rocks, stones, ponds and lakes have the potential to become Buddhas. Thought forms duplicate the same process for materialization. You first think an idea into the thought form. The thought attains the constituency of light in its respective dimension. The

Caylor Adkins performing the first move, from the kata called Jion.

whole begins to build up by attracting molecular particles of ether, which gives substance to materialization. You have now initiated the creation of something from cause and effect. Nikola Tesla was experimenting with a similar concept to attempt to tap into the earth's natural magnetic field to create free energy.

This is one of the most important secrets of the universe for humans to understand and control in the most positive way. Whatever you concentrate on and think about most your mind will create. If you think about what you don't want too much, that is what your mind will create ... what you don't want. This is the creative part of God and the universe, which is built into our minds. Most people do not succeed to the level that they want, because they think about what they are worried about too much. They think about their desires and goals, but they equally think about how concerned they are about them not happening. That causes a major resistance in the mind. It is like putting your foot on the gas and the brake pedal at the same time. This is also why many of peoples' prayers do not materialize. They pray very focused and intensely, but their numerous worries and concerns come into their minds and they pray that they won't happen.

Caylor Adkins attacking an opponent at Ed Parker's International Tournament in Long Beach, California, in the early 1960's.

Then they think and contemplate too much about what they are going to do if it doesn't happen.

You have the ability to create in form anything you can think or conceive of and produce the right action to materialize it. For your benefit, you almost have to keep a "gate guardian" at the entrance of your mind to control what you let in. If you catch yourself thinking something negative, quickly distract yourself from thinking those thoughts with something positive. The quality of your thoughts can affect your strength and endurance levels. If you are in a depressed mental state, it will drastically weaken your abilities. Thoughts will have an affect on the digestion of your food. Thoughts will also have an affect on how you heal from an injury or a disease. Your mind is like a garden. You must continually plant and weed it.

You have to be careful how you ask yourself questions in your mind. If you say, "Why can't I find this?", "Why can't I make enough money?", "Why can't I get better?", "Why can't I get stronger?" or "Why can't I fight better?" your mind will find thousands of reasons through your subconscious why you can't do these things. The attached act of wanting something out of an insecure mentality can actually push it away from you. If you want success out of that insecure mental state, your mind will create a situation in which you want the continued state of wanting success, but you will never get it.

There is an old saying, "If you chase after the universe, it will run away from you. If you run away from the universe, it will run after you." Change your reality. Just a simple change in words can make a world of difference. Try saying, "How can I become a better fighter?", "How can I get better?" or "How can I make more money?" Whatever you put in your subconscious mind usually explores and expands. If you ask yourself all of the negative reasons why you don't do something, it will answer you with all of the negative answers. If you ask for the positive answers to help correct your problem or situations, your mind will work on that and give them to you.

You also have to be careful of what you ask your subconscious mind to do, because there is a good chance you might get it. You have to analyze whether what you asked for is really going to be good for you. If you get your subconscious mind to experience abundance, it will create that. Then you can be the creation of your own cause and not someone else's.

Many people have problems accomplishing their goals, because their conscious mind wants one thing and their subconscious mind wants something different. For example, if an individual wants to be a public speaker, but subconsciously has a fear of being in front of an audience, his subconscious mind will find a way to sabotage that achievement. If an individual wants to be a fighter but subconsciously has a fear of getting hurt, his subconscious mind will find a way to sabotage that ... until he gets rid of the fear. You must train the conscious and subconscious mind to become one in your endeavors. You must learn how to align your conscious and subconscious mind on the same belief system. Then you will have a fuller power of mind to work with. If there are contradictions in your training, relationships and life, there are contradictions between your conscious and subconscious minds. Whenever you mentally resist something too much, you can become attached too it. This recipe can give what you are resisting more power and it can sometimes imbed itself deeper into your subconscious mind. Everything you are against can then weaken you. Everything you are for can strengthen you. If you reject something passionately, it is saying it doesn't exist as part of you. It is better to mentally rise above both. There is a big difference between being and doing. The subconscious mind searches being, not just doing. Being attracts beingness, which produces experience.

Most people are programmed to think before they act. If you really want to change your thought, act before you think. Move on your first impulse. Act before your mind kills the new ideas and talks you out of it. This is the fastest way to change your thoughts. First, just do the action, which equals what you want to do or change. Then say the words, which equal the action. Then think the thoughts, which equal the word. If you procrastinate in your training, don't think about what you are going to do and over plan it. Just do the physical action, even if it is only 10 times.

One of my original senior karate instructors was Caylor Adkins, who started training in the mid-1950's and became one of Tsutomu Ohshima's original six black belts. He used to tell us, "Don't be concerned about executing and accomplishing 500 front kicks when you want to start a practice." He said, "Just say you're going to do 10 and by then you won't be able to stop there. You'll want to do 50, then 100 and so on."

Caylor was also the one who introduced to us the Chinese iron ball concepts. He got these from his brother, Curtis, a Chinese martial artist. Curtis spent a lot of time studying in China and this practice involved utilizing an 8-pound shot-put. You

*Caylor Adkins blocking a thrust-kick, executed
by Sadaharu Honda in the mid-1960's.*

would duplicate the circular and figure-eight patterns of many boxing punches with the shot-put in your hands. You alternate hands and patterns, keeping your body flowing from its core. This technique and practice is still not well known. Caylor recently wrote a book on specialized training with the iron ball, staff and boxing concepts. These principles hold the secret of connecting your mind-body and breathing as one unit. If you execute a continuous (ki) type of breathing with the flowing movements, you instantly get into a peak performance mental state. This is one of the best exercises and training methods to develop the core of your body. It is especially beneficial using this breathing and iron ball movement to create a mind and body oneness. You could more easily control your thoughts in this mental state.

With some effort you can change any negative habitual thought pattern with this practice. The best tools to create what you want to in your mind are thoughts, words, deeds and actions. You must continually control your thoughts, because they become words. Control your words, because they become actions. Control your actions, because they become habits. Control your habits, because they become your character. Control your character, because it becomes your destiny.

I remember hearing a story when I was in the Special Forces in the military. Two S.F. soldiers were escaping from an ambush through a thick jungle in a foreign country. Rebels were shooting at them through their initial escape. Eventually, they lost the rebels, after they had traveled a few kilometers through the jungle. Both soldiers knelt down on one knee. The soldier on the right put his left hand on the other soldier's right shoulder blade and said, "I think we lost them." He then pulled his hand away and saw it was all covered with blood. He realized that his team member got hit with a bullet. His team member didn't even notice in the excitement of the firefight with the adrenaline and endorphins pumping. The soldier with the blood on his hand didn't want to startle his friend and knew it was important not to express how bad it was. So, he decided to tell him by saying, "It looks like you got hit a little bit." The hit team member responded, "What do you mean hit a little bit? How can you get hit a little bit?" Right after he saw all the blood on his friend's hand from his wound, he passed out. Before this, he didn't even realize he was shot. He let negative thoughts into his mind, after realizing he was hit, and made himself pass out.

Key Points

- Keep a gate guardian at the entrance to your mind to monitor your thoughts.
- Observe and eliminate the amount of negative thinking you do.

- Practice distraction to help eliminate negative thoughts.
- Attempt to keep the majority of your thoughts very positive, no matter what the subject is.
- Practice total mindfulness in your thinking. Keep all your energy focused in your present moment.
- You are the most important person you can have a positive mental conversation with.
- Always talk to yourself positively. Never talk down to yourself.
- The more energy you give your thoughts, the more they will expand. Plus thoughts will expand and so will minus thoughts. Keep your thoughts positive.
- Ask yourself questions in a very positive way to get productive answers and results. Don't ask yourself questions in a way that you only get negative answers.
- Whatever you put in your subconscious mind, your subconscious mind will explore and expand on.
- Make yourself experience abundance in your mind and your subconscious mind will help create it.
- There are contradictions in your life, because there are contradictions in your mind.
- You must continually practice aligning your conscious and subconscious mind on matters to get the results you want.
- If you want to help change your thought patterns, act before you think, rather than think before you act.

Chapter 9

Positive Self-Controlling Attitude

With the exception of one thing, everything can be taken away from us. We can have our finances, house, job, friends and all of our material things taken away. The one thing, which can never be taken away from us, unless we choose to let it? Our attitude!

We choose to give away our attitude all of the time. When we get hurt, upset, mad or depressed, we give away the state of our attitude. No one takes it; we choose to let it degrade. We can make up every excuse possible as to why this situation made us hurt, mad or depressed. The bottom line, however, is that we caved into letting that happen. We also have the power and will in our consciousness to decide what our attitude is going to be, no matter what we experience. If an individual wants to have the attitude of a warrior, he has to train himself to be in control of his attitude no matter what the circumstances. We could go through one of the most traumatic experiences in life and still have the ability to face it with the best attitude. And, any positive elements we can learn from it would be for the betterment of our character. In such a tragic situation, there might be only positive ele-

*Don Depree pushing himself to the ultimate degree, while he
is leading Special Training and practicing kata in the ocean.*

ments totaling 2 percent; nevertheless, a true warrior will focus
on that 2 percent and not the 98 percent.

We can choose how we decide to experience every moment
in our training, job, profession, business, relationships and life.
Every moment in life is a very special moment. Each experience
in life always has a hidden treasure. You just have to find it. Don't
wait for special moments in life; create them. We usually are programmed to feel bad whenever something negative happens to
us. The main problem is that when we do feel down, negative or
depressed it doesn't help the situation at all. It just makes it worse
until we actually decide to not be down or depressed anymore.
We are usually waiting for something outside, as a trigger, to feel
better about a situation. We don't have to wait for that trigger;
we have the power and will to decide anytime to help us feel bet-

ter and more positive. All we have to do is have the mental strength, desire, will and commitment to choose it.

A positive attitude finds better ways to accomplish something. A negative mind only finds excuses. It takes less energy to be positive, and it drains you of energy to be negative. It takes 72 muscles to frown, but only 14 muscles to smile. When you keep yourself in distress or hell, you are unable to experience who you really are. Failure is an event; it is not a person. When there is hope in the future, there is power in today. If you truly want to be happy, don't wait for something to happen to be happy. Decide today to be happy ... right now. Happiness is a conscious act. It is here and now. Not a where and when. It is a conscious choice. Not, "I'll be happy when this happens." Fun and games do not bring true happiness. Accomplishing challenges and getting through turmoil help bring true happiness and build character with the appropriate mentality. You must control how you choose to experience your life. A true warrior usually picks the most difficult way, but he gains the most.

Three billion people go to bed somewhere in the world very hungry every night. There are four billion people who go to bed every night, deprived of love, support and encouragement. People will do anything to get love, support and encouragement. They will even become terrorists and blow themselves up to get support and encouragement from their contemporaries. Statistics reveal that 44 percent of people quit something because they don't feel appreciated. The majority of people on the planet are totally motivated in their lives by attempting to get love, respect, support, endorsement and encouragement from other people. These individuals attempt to work from the outside in. A true warrior works from inside of himself and then proceeds out. He finds an expression in life that he can identify with from the deepest core of his mind. Most of the people on the planet do or become something to please other people, and not necessarily themselves. The warrior finds a passion, a definite purpose to express himself in life. This is his mission in life, and he goes at it with a single-minded purpose.

Years ago, researchers followed a number of people with high IQs until they became very successful. The common denominator for these people is that they picked one subject in life they were passionate about and did something every day to further their knowledge toward a goal of mastering their subject. You must back fate with action. If you want more in life, become more in life. Just create it. Be very careful of most people's opinions, as they are usually very biased.

Nature naturally multiplies like a crop. So does success with the appropriate positive attitude. There is a fixed pattern of nature, the planets and stars. Man can create a pattern for success. You must always associate with winners in life or individuals with higher mentality. Continually associate with more successful people with positive attitudes ... not negative people or losers. Individuals usually achieve success to the extent that they have failed in the past. A person with a positive attitude will never give up. He may investigate another way to accomplish something, but he will never give up. Your attitude affects everyone and everything around you like a magnet. Most people can usually tell what your attitude is, even before you speak, by the way you walk and carry yourself. This is particularly true with a warrior. He can always tell if his opponent is self-confident or insecure and what his weaknesses are. It is even hard for disease to live in a body with a very strong positive attitude. The right positive attitude can help heal you faster, as your subconscious mind will continually look for more effective ways to progress your healing. If you really have a serious problem, instead of being totally focused on yourself and solving your problem, it is better to find a person with a similar problem and help him.

Four-fifths of the people on the planet are conditioned to believe that life is a trial or test. You can make it a test or a trial if you like, but you will never fully realize your true potential, mission and destiny in life. A warrior creates personal tests and trials

Don Depree and Henry Wilkerson fighting each other
at a (dan) test or senior black belt grading in 1976.

all the time, only to further expand his potential. Your life's true mission is a process of creative evolution and understanding. Life is not a process of trying to discover who you are. It is a process of creation of who you already are and expanding on that.

On a spiritual level, most are actually trying to remember who they are. Most created themselves to experience who they really are. Thus, create who you really are and then experience it. Knowing and experiencing something is a totally different level. The soul's evolutionary process is knowing, experiencing and then being. Each soul picks its own destiny for its quickest remembering. You either choose to remember who you already are or you go through life trying to find yourself when you're already there. The best way to accomplish this is to experience what you are until you experience what you are not. God, or the creator, can't experience himself being the creator until he can experience himself creating. Humans must also experience themselves creating in life. Heaven will not do anything for you that you will not do for yourself. If you are truly God's equal, nothing is being done to you. You are creating everything around you like God is. You can't believe in God or the universe unless you totally believe in yourself. When you totally accept the responsibility for doing something, then you have the power to change it. If you stay in denial, make excuses and blame everyone else, you give your power away to change it. The subconscious mind gravitates towards connection, harmony and unity with all things, just like God is experiencing himself. When you become very biased and condemn something, you are condemning a part of yourself in your higher consciousness. Everything you do to other people you do to yourself, positive or negative. If you hurt other people, you can actually hurt yourself with a certain attitude. The soul's real purpose is just to self-realize.

A warrior must be the creation of his own cause in life. The process goes something like this: the soul conceives the mind, the mind creates the body and the body creates its experiences. We are spiritual beings having a human experience ... not human beings having a spiritual experience. Enlightenment is accepting what we have and where we are at right now in life.

It is very easy for many people to misinterpret this next statement. God's greatest gift is your realization you don't need God. If you are expressing and experiencing your life from your higher consciousness, you are channeling God's will and being. You then don't have to find God. If you acquire this kind of understanding, it will definitely affect the type of attitude you have in your life.

One I've always admired as an excellent example of always

displaying a great positive attitude in life, is Don DePree. He is one of Tsutomu Ohshima's senior black belts and has trained for about 45 years. I've noticed through the years, no matter what type of serious personal problems he has, he always asks how you are doing. He automatically puts all of his attention on you and not him at all. It doesn't seem like much for most people, but I have never heard him complain about anything or anybody, no matter how serious it was. You would never know. He never lowers himself to get involved in small or negative talk. I seriously believe that if I called him and he had a spear and three bullets in his chest, I would never know, unless I really pressed it. He would again first ask me how I am doing and ask how all of my projects are going. When I asked, "How are you doing and feeling?" He would say, "Fine." If I actually found out that he had a spear in his chest and showed concern, he would say, "I'm fine and I'll be alright." I know this seems exaggerated and there is a time to let friends and people know you need help. He is a phenomenal example of a true warrior with an incredibly strong mind who truly exhibits a great positive mentality in everything he does and everyone he associates with.

I have to mention another example of how a strong positive mentality can benefit your life in a critical situation. There was an individual named Jim who worked at an insurance company. He studied every positive attitude and thinking book he could put his hands on. He would continually apply the principals at work successfully. He had a dream of going into business for himself and raising enough money to open a chain of jeweler stores. In a year he finally opened his first store. In a couple years, he had three of them and was very successful.

One night late he was at the office of his main store doing some extra paperwork. He suddenly realized he didn't lock the back door of the store. He started to run over there, but it was too late. Two robbers were already coming in the back door with guns. Jim pleaded with the robbers and told them that they could take anything they wanted, but don't hurt him, as he had a wife and two children. The robbers gathered everything they could carry, but then they heard a siren go off. One of the robbers panicked, ran over to Jim and pointed the gun at him. The robber thought the siren was a police car approaching. Jim again pleaded with the robber not to shoot him. This time it didn't help. The robber shot him three times in the chest.

Jim became conscious again on a gurney, being rolled into the emergency room at a hospital. He felt a burning fire in his chest. He didn't know how bad he was, but he knew he could tell by looking up at the expressions on the faces of the nurses and doctors around him. When he got their attention, he looked up and just saw the face of death on everyone. He got the feeling they were going to operate on him like he was going to die anyway. He knew he had to do something to change their attitude and the atmosphere. After everything he studied about positive thinking, there had to be something. While they were questioning him, as they started to operate on him, Jim knew this was his last chance. Then a doctor got to this question. "Jim, are you allergic to anything?" Jim thought for a moment and answered, "Yes, there is one thing, BULLETS!" Everyone paused for a moment and couldn't believe it. They all started laughing, which created the positive attitude. The doctors felt they had to save this guy and they did.

Key Points
- We truly have total control over one thing in our life and that is attitude.
- We have the power and will to decide to make our attitude better at anytime we want.
- A positive mind finds ways to accomplish and achieve things. A negative mind only finds excuses.

- Failure is an event, not a person.
- When there is hope in the future, there is power in today.
- Adversity, experiencing turmoil and getting through them with the appropriate attitude builds character.
- Life is a process of who you are, creating and expanding on that.
- The soul's real purpose is to self-realize.
- Enlightenment is accepting what we have and where we are in life right now.

Chapter 10

Unyielding Self-Confidence

There are many facets to building stronger self-confidence. Those include having great ability, techniques, tactics, strategy and accomplishing numerous challenging goals. A strong belief in you, along with positive achievement experiences, will add to it. There is a theory that we are born genetically with a certain amount of self-confidence. There is also a definite difference between egotism and strong self-confidence. We must have a balance between the two or we could easily be perceived as being too self-conscious even selfish. Many times a person with a big ego, who hasn't gone through intense training, will get very egotistical and boastful. He will start thinking and bragging that he can do and has done many things, even if he hasn't. He will exaggerate his accomplishments and goals. His thoughts will be filtered and exaggerated through his ego, and he will perceive the world through that ego. This type of mentality will throw his center, balance and perception of himself off. He will not be able to see and look at himself clearly. This will also affect the way he pushes himself and his whole training program. A real warrior has to be strict, look at himself clearly and see the truth. The true warrior's real and worst opponent is when he has to face himself. He must know his strengths and weaknesses. If he wants to become stronger and more self-confident, he must be honest with himself. Most people either overlook, or are biased away from recognizing their weaknesses and shortcomings. This understanding tends to build self confidence on false premises. This is also why it is especially important for a warrior to be as humble, as he is self-confident. The stronger a warrior becomes mentally, technically and physically, the more humility he should also acquire. This humility is not only projected to others, but also to himself. The more strength a warrior acquires, the less he has to prove himself. Eventually, he doesn't have to prove himself at all. Many times a true warrior will not be perceived as strong and tough. When an average person finds out who this person is, what he has done, been through and accomplished, he will be shocked, because the person seemed so unassuming. Most people will not recognize this person as a warrior, until a critical situation arises and the warrior steps up and does what he has to do.

An important element of building confidence is taken for granted, because it is so simple. Living up to your word. You are as strong and confident as your word. When you say you are going to do something, you do it or don't say it. Of course, there is a sensitive balance to be aware of here, too. You must first be careful of what you give your word to do. You also may have to depend on a lot of other people, which will affect your ability to keep your word. As I mentioned earlier, a true warrior looks at himself with strict eyes. You may be able to fool other people, but if you observe yourself with these strict eyes, you will not be able to fool yourself. That is the most important element. You cannot fool your subconscious mind, because you really know the truth. Every time you do not follow through with your word, your mind files it in your subconscious like an uncompleted task. Doing this for an extended period of time, builds a big weakness in your mind. When you do this, you are continually building up a pattern in the deeper part of your mind that you don't follow through with your word. That definitely affects your inner confidence in the deeper part of your mind. When you have to reach deep down for that core confidence, a critical situation, it will not be there. When you continuously follow through with your word, you are subconsciously and successfully completing a project. The more you do that, the stronger your word and commitment will become, because you have conditioned it. This in turn will continually build a greater self-confidence that cannot be thwarted.

As I mentioned in a previous chapter, you have to be careful how you talk to yourself when you build stronger confidence. You must talk to yourself respectfully. Do not ever talk down to yourself, as it will degrade your confidence. If you make a mistake, don't criticize yourself too harshly. Just think of how you can rectify and better the situation for everyone involved and do it. Don't wallow being down, depressed and beat yourself up about it. You can have more confidence in your training and

Tom Muzila in his mountain man days, exhibiting inner strength and strong confidence from his training.

your life by asking yourself better questions. If you want to improve your abilities, you have to ask yourself questions in a more positive way. For example, "Why can't I get better at this technique?" A slight change puts the problem in a more positive state. "What can I do and how can I train to get better at this technique?" Now you are not talking down to yourself, such as when you ask, "Why can't I?" When you do this, your mind will find a thousand reasons why you can't. When you have a negative training period, find the positive elements that you acquired from the practice. If you only discover what not to do, that is still positive. Don't let anything or anyone tear you down or degrade you. Program yourself not to complain, make excuses or even engage in small talk. Continually ask yourself positive, accomplishing questions in the morning when you get up and just before you go to sleep. This will keep you on track. Proper positive dialogue and questions to yourself will help build a more confident subconscious mind.

An appropriate balance of self-confidence and humility, will drastically affect your life and everyone and everything around you.

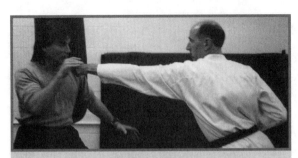

Tom Muzila teaching Doug Podkin, an F-16 Jet Pilot, a karate technique. Doug found that developing more confidence through karate positively networked over to his abilities as a jet pilot.

You will make others feel very comfortable being with you. They will sense your strong self-confidence. You will create a positive magnetism around you. Sometimes people will push you into a leadership position formally or informally. Many people are attracted to a person with strong self-confidence. If you are a business or professional person, people can easily tell if you are confident in your job, position and in your product or service. You must know yourself first, inside and out, and then your product. If you know your product thoroughly but not yourself, people will eventually figure it out. You won't be able to successfully sell anything to anyone else, unless you are totally self-confident and believe in yourself. People can tell if you are really self-confident in your beliefs. As a warrior, the most important element is for your opponent to know you are confident in yourself and your abilities. If you are insecure, he can tell by the way you carry yourself, talk and move. It shows in your subconscious body movement and in your eyes. A strong opponent will know. There is a fixed pattern to nature. You can create a pattern in your training and life to develop a strong habitual self-confidence. If you have developed a strong self-confidence, you can control your opponent and situations in life, by virtue of your own mind.

In 1964, Tsutomu Ohshima was in the lobby of a Los Angeles hotel before a big karate instructors' meeting with Caylor Adkins, one of his senior black belts. There were about 200 black belts there, many tough and strong looking individuals. Then, a small, light-framed Chinese-looking individual walked through the lobby. No one else even noticed him. Ohshima Sensei bumped Caylor's arm and said, "That is one of the best martial artist in this room." No one else knew him at the time and neither did Ohshima Sensei. That individual was Bruce Lee. Ohshima could tell—by the way he carried himself, his body movement and confidence—that he was a very well trained martial artist.

Key Points

- A strong belief in yourself and your abilities will help build better self-confidence.
- Your perception of reality and life is filtered through your mentality.
- You must develop the proper balance between self-confidence and humility.
- A true warrior doesn't have to prove himself.
- You must look at yourself and criticize yourself with strict eyes.
- The warrior's worst opponent is himself.
- You are as strong and confident as your word.
- Always talk to yourself very respectfully.
- Ask yourself positive and productive questions related to everything.
- Never let anything degrade you mentally.
- Never make excuses. Always take responsibility for your actions.
- Know yourself first and then know your product or service.
- People can tell if you are self-confident and believe in yourself.
- A strong opponent can easily know if you are self-confident.
- Your self-confidence is displayed from your subconscious mind ... the way you walk, talk and carry yourself. It also shows in your eyes.
- You can control your opponent and situations in your life by the virtue and the self-confidence you have in your mind.

Chapter 11

Developing Focus and Mental Strength

S ome individuals seem naturally born with mental strength. They can apply it to some elements in life but sometimes not to others. Everyone, including you, can develop stronger focus and mental strength. All you have to do is continually practice exercises that will expand on the intensity and duration of your focus and mental strength.

A true warrior takes it to the next step. He develops a more intense and longer duration of his focus and mental strength under an extreme amount of stress and even life-and-death situations.

Optimum focus and mental strength do not come from external facial and body tension, but from internal sources: practicing to hold a thought longer and being more mentally intense and deeper ... without anything distracting you, including pain.

If two high-level martial artists or karate-ka face each other in a fight, the one who will win will be the one holds his focus, concentration and mental strength a little longer than his opponent. When his opponent has a split second gap in concentration, he will attack and take advantage. That will determine the result of the fight. There have been numerous stories throughout history in which an older, more experienced warrior—with incredible focus, concentration and mental strength—defeated a talented, younger warrior with less focus simply because his concentration was better.

Tsutomu Ohshima once told us about a man he met in Europe who had the strongest and most concentrated, intense eyes he'd ever seen. He found out later that the man hunted Bengal tigers with only a short wooden staff with a carved point on the end in India for many years. The man was an Indian silk warrior. He would make himself totally vulnerable to the tiger's environment and get the tiger to attack him. He would then take a strong stance and place the bottom of the short five-foot staff in front of his back foot, while pointing the sharp end at the tiger. When the tiger would lunge to attack him, the man would extend the staff into the tiger's throat ... as the tigers claws wrapped around him. The Indian warrior would stare right into the tiger's eyes to the end. Mr. Ohshima said the man had killed numerous tigers that way, but he did have many scars around his back and shoulders from the tigers clawing him.

It has been a practice of some of the top warriors in history to study the gaze and stare from ferocious wild animals. If you practice looking deep into the eyes of a tiger, lion, wolf, gorilla or water buffalo, you will immediately understand what true focus and concentration is. All these animals, and many more, have a natural instinct for killing. They don't even think about it. It is excellent training to practice gazing into the eyes of these beasts as long as you can without wavering. The eyes are the lamps of the soul. You can see all of one's strengths and weakness by gazing into the eyes. The samurai had an old saying, "When a cat stares at a mouse, the mouse forgets about his feet." If the mouse is standing or running across a beam and looks down to catch the eyes of a cat, he will fall and the cat will get him. Mr. Ohshima made another saying popular. "Speed is eyes and power is hips."

Before you have strong and concentrated eyes, you have to

train yourself to have a strong and focused and concentrated mind. The mind has the capacity to focus and concentrate incredibly deeply. Only a small percentage of individuals have taken the mind to these deeper concentrated levels. Your mind controls your spirit and your spirit controls your body. You must first practice to acquire total mindfulness and awareness of every moment. A much fuller capacity of your mind is only focused on the present moment or second. Then the next moment and the next second. When you are able to

Tsutomu Ohshima demonstrating how his punching power can penetrate through two people. He has also accomplished it with three people.

generate an incredibly strong focus, everything in your mind will slow things down around you. Many individuals experience this when they have a life-threatening experience. Everything around them slows down in their mind.

When you are able to do this, your mind will naturally focus at such extreme depths, out of some survival instinct, that it will look like everything is moving in slow motion. If you develop a very strong mentality, you can do this at will. When you have this kind of a strong mind or mentality, your speed becomes quicker and you see everything around you more clearly. If you can concentrate with a strong mind and focus, it will connect a feeling to your lower abdomen. When you are able to connect your concentration to your lower abdomen, you will be able to have a more grounded and centered connection with the earth or floor. This is one of the main energy centers a warrior focuses from when he engages in battle. It is the center and spoke of the

Bill Ungerman hammering a nail through a piece of wood, which requires extreme concentration and focus.

wheel from where the body will concentrate. The warrior will naturally lower his hips and will be more connected to the ground.

When you acquire this type of strong, concentrated, focused mentality, your mind easily speeds up its destiny. It already has executed its mission. If you are facing an opponent, it is not in the mode of, "I will get him or hit him." It is in the mode that I already have hit or gotten him in your mind. The physical just has to catch up to the mental, which it will, if you are facing a weaker or less focused opponent.

Miyamoto Musashi, one of the world's greatest samurai of the 1600 century, had a swordsmanship school later in his life. He wrote the strategy book called, The Book of Five Rings, during the last two years of his life while he lived in a cave. Translated, the name of his swordsmanship school was, "The Rock." The lord of that province once visited Musashi and was confused why Musashi called his swordsmanship school this. Musashi said, "I will show you." He called over one of his top senior pupils and told him, "The lord has requested that you commit seppuku (which is hari-kari or disembowelment). The lord really didn't say that, but Musashi wanted to demonstrate a specific focused and totally concentrated mentality, even in the face of death. Musashi's senior student didn't make any excuses, complain or even display any shock or surprise in the lord's request. He just asked, "Please give me a few moments to prepare myself with the proper ritual and attire." He showed no change at all in his expression or mentality. He was ready for death at any moment. Just before Musashi's senior student was ready to stick himself with his tanto (short knife), Musashi told his senior student that the lord changed his mind and he didn't have to commit hara-kiri. His senior member's expression once again didn't change or act relived at all. He just mentioned, "May I go back to training?" Musashi said, "Yes!" The lord finally understood why Musashi selected that name. The student's mind didn't move at all, whether faced with death by his own hand or after given life; he wasn't overjoyed. The student's mind didn't move. That is an optimum example of focus and deep concentration.

There is a concept in Japanese called "kime," and it takes an entire paragraph in English to properly explain it. It is basically an ability to direct all your intense strength, energy and concentration in one specific moment at the optimum time to generate maximum power. It takes extreme concentration and training to move decisively at the most advantageous moment. It is one thing to just develop and be able to generate this type of intense focus, but you also have to implement it at the exact time and moment with the most advantageous technique. You also have to be able to execute this with the optimum mental and physical body state. How do you practice to develop basic focus and concentration? The training concept is very simple. You first have to be able to think about one thing and just continually practice to hold that thought in your mind without wavering. Then you have to train yourself to mentally hold that focus and concentration deeper and longer, without being distracted by anything. The ultimate state would be to hold it even in the face of death and still not waver.

It is incredible how this type of intense concentrated focus can influence your speed, power and technical level. Ron McNair was a physicist and scientist. He was one of the astronauts who unfortunately perished in the Challenger Shuttle disaster in 1986. He was a very serious martial artist. At the time he perished in the Shuttle disaster, he was a fifth-degree black belt. He also made a serious scientific study of karate by measuring how certain aspects of speed and power were concentrated. During his studies, he and a couple other colleagues began an intensive study of the physical forces involved in karate. They first found that a karate punch executed from an expert takes .15 seconds to compete and produces 100 joules of energy. That is enough energy to lift a one-pound weight more than 70 feet. They also found that a perfectly executed technique reaches a speed of seven meters per second. He discovered that most karate techniques are automatically focused beyond and through the target to generate the maximum amount of power. His studies proved that a punch produced the maximum delivery of energy at about 1.5 inches before the arm was fully extended. McNair's research team also measured the force and the time required for breaking. They noted that it only took one-tenth of the available energy needed to smash a two-inch thick concrete slab. They also discovered it was 100 times harder to break the bones of someone in a good, strong concentrated karate defensive posture than it was to break wood or concrete slabs. The main results of the study revealed that these ancient karate and martial artist designers knew what they were doing, because they are so scientifically sound. McNair stated, "We haven't discovered anything. We just have a chance to discover what these ancient masters already knew and have known for centuries by intuition."

Dar Robinson was one of the greatest stuntman and stunt coordinators in the history of films. He originally set many records in all types of stunts, and he had incredible physical, technical and mental abilities. His focus and concentration were phenomenal. Unfortunately, he was killed years ago in a motorcycle accident.

Years before, he performed a stunt, a first of its kind. He

jumped and did a freefall off the Toronto Tower with only a small descender cable hooked to his back. It was engineered with a braking system that would be applied the last few feet before he hit the ground. Kathy Lee Crosby hosted the event. Initially, the stunt had to be postponed for a few days, because it was so windy. When they tested the braking system a couple days before he was going to do the jump, it failed and a 150-pound bag of sand cratered into the ground. Dar had faced death many times throughout his career, but he couldn't wait any longer. A few moments before he sat on the edge of the Tower he walked up to his good friend, Frank, who

Bill Ungerman demonstrating mental focus, while shooting. Bill experienced two tours of Viet Nam, Force Recon Marines and 173rd Ranger Battalion.

was the main engineer for all of his stunts. He told Frank, "If it fails and I crater into the ground, please don't blame yourself. Also, if that happens and I crater into the ground, I'm keeping my eyes open all the way. I want to face death until he last second." A few moments later, he jumped and the stunt was a total success.

There are two basic ways to practice mental focus and concentration techniques. One is to meditate with the eyes closed and the other is to meditate with the eyes open. This can be harder, because you can become more distracted from all of the external elements around you. A popular meditation technique in Zen is to have your eyes closed and not think or concentrate on any thoughts. Keep your mind totally empty. When a thought comes up, don't build on it, just let it go until you can consistently quiet your mind down and acquire what is referred to as a "no mind or nothingness" mentality. If you can practice to consistently acquire this state of mind, when you actually focus on a thought, you will automatically be able to concentrate on it deeper and longer. When meditating with your eyes open, the trick is to acquire a strong focus so that you don't blink at all for a long period of time. It doesn't matter whether you are meditating on an object or gazing out into space. When you acquire a deeper focus, you will more easily be able to not blink and keep your eyes open. That ability will help you to achieve a more concentrated mental state whenever you need it.

Key Points

- Everyone can practice to attain focus and concentration that are deeper, more intense and longer.
- If you have two experienced fighters, the survivor will usually be the one with the most unshakable focus and concentration.
- A true warrior can hold his focus without wavering, even if he is facing a ferocious animal.
- The eyes are the lamps of the soul.
- Speed is eyes and power is hips.
- Practice total mindfulness and awareness of each moment.
- Everything will slow down around you in your mind if you acquire an extremely deep focus and concentration. This usually happens in life-threatening experiences.
- When you have strong focus, your speed will become quicker and your mind clearer.

- If you have an extremely strong mental state and focus, you will not think and feel, "I will hit my opponent." Instead, you have already hit your opponent in your mind.
- You can develop such incredible mental strength that your mind will be like a rock and not even waver, in the face of death.
- Practice to generate, focus and develop your kime and be able to use it, whenever you need to in life.
- Continually practice meditating, so you can develop a no-thought, no-mind, or nothingness mental state at will.

Chapter 12

Dynamic Imagery
and Visualization

I magery and visualization are some of the oldest mental techniques existing in human history. They will enhance your performance in fighting, sports, your career, relationships and all arts. This has been scientifically tested for many years. Anyone who mentally rehearses the performance he is going to do many times before the event will perform at a much higher level. The concepts have evolved incredibly and are now foolproof and sophisticated. The benefits of practiced imagery have been exhibited in all aspects of life, including relationships, job performance and productivity. Visualization has also been known to aid self-confidence, self-esteem, positive thinking, and having a more positive and productive attitude.

Think of the process as comparable to watching a video. In life, we get whatever we primarily prepare for the majority of time. Whatever picture or activity we continually keep playing in our mind over and over again will eventually materialize. This picture or visual film can be motivated by fear or insecurities, and the outcome can be negative or positive. This is why it is important to monitor what you picture in your mind. It is very impor-

*Senior Tadao Okuyama demonstrates bokken techniques
with an opponent. Visualize beating your opponent
with an attack, way before the engagement.*

tant to determine the source of your visualizations, as well as the mentality or attitude motivating them.

Be careful what goals you decide to achieve. When you plant a seed in your subconscious mind with enough motivation and desire, your subconscious mind will continually work on it. The best part about this mental phenomenon is that we can use it to our advantage to help us acquire what we want to achieve.

Here are some points to keep in mind when you are visualizing or practicing imagery. Your mind is like a huge iceberg. The visible tip of the iceberg, is your conscious mind. The huge part, which you don't see, is under the water and at least 10 times bigger. This is your subconscious mind. If your subconscious mind is trained and programmed properly, it is incredibly powerful. As mentioned, it can work in a positive or negative way for you. Your subconscious mind doesn't know the difference between the future, past or present. You can use this element to your advantage. We have all heard through our lives, that the majority of people only use about five percent of their brain capacity. The majority of people do not take the time to develop themselves mentally. Most people tend to focus the bigger amount of time on developing themselves externally. This is one of the main reasons why they don't utilize more.

The hardest part of programming or training your subconscious mind is getting it to accept affirmations. Under the right conditions and state of mind, it doesn't matter what your affirmations are; your subconscious mind will accept them. The secret of getting your subconscious mind to accept affirmations is being in an alpha state of mind when you program it. That is the state of mind in which your brain waves are flowing from seven to 13 hertz cycles per second. The beta state of mind is 13 and above hertz cycles per second, a very awake and conscious mental state. The alpha state is basically a relaxed but awakened state of mind. We go in and out of the alpha state of mind many times a day, as when we listen to, pleasant music or when we relax and stare off into the clouds or beautiful scenery.

The best way to get in this state is to consciously relax your body and focus on each body part. This will help you to relax deeply and take all of the tension out of each limb and portion of your body. The more your body is able to relax, the more your mind is able to relax. It also goes the other way around. When you can calm your mind, your body will be more apt to follow. The best way to relax and calm your mind is through breathing. Take bigger breaths and execute longer exhales. Feel the tension excreting out of your body with every exhale.

There are many other ways to achieve the alpha state, such as listening to nature's sounds, including a waterfall, rain, a creek or even crickets at night. Other sounds are called "pink" or "white noise." This sounds like static on a radio or TV. Sometimes just calming down and mentally visualizing a very peaceful scene in your mind will also automatically do it.

Most people program their subconscious minds incorrectly.

As mentioned, the subconscious mind doesn't really know the difference between the past, present or future. If you tell your subconscious mind, "I will become a better martial artist,or I will make more money," this can put your subconscious mind in a continuous cycle of always striving to become better and always trying to make more money.

"I am" is the most powerful statement you can make to yourself as you add on to whatever you desire. This statement programs your subconscious mind to be already making more "money" immediately. In reality, even if it isn't, the subconscious mind is much more powerfully programmed to have something. It will work more positively and efficiently at acquiring what it is already supposed to have. A better example of an affirmation would be, "I am a stronger and smarter fighter." The more specific you can be, the more skilled you will be in that one specific ability or technique. The focus your subconscious mind puts out to very broad affirmations will be more dispersed. When you are specific in your affirmations, it directs the majority of your energy toward making that one specific ability or technique better. Nothing is wrong with general affirmations, but you have to combine them with specific ones, as well.

Too many affirmations, of course, can disperse your focus over too broad a field where it gets lost in the underbrush. A good way to integrate your general affirmation with your specific ones would be to have one general one, such as, "I am a stronger and smarter fighter." Then have two or no more than three specific technique affirmations to branch out from the general one. The specific ones could be, "I have a very fast and powerful offensive front kick." The other could be, " I have a precisely timed defensive reverse punch, which I make effective every time."

You can put this portion of the program together in the following manner. Get yourself in a very relaxed physical and mental state, using your long deep breathing. Now start saying to yourself, even out loud, your first general affirmation over and over again. The more focused and concentrated you can get yourself, the better. You may have to say the affirmation to yourself 10 times, which is fine. You can also do the same with the more specific affirmations, too. Before we get into this part, we are going to add a whole new dimension to the affirmations, which will be like adding a turbo charger to programming your subconscious mind properly. We are going to add the visual and imagery portion to your affirmations.

The visual and imagery portion of programming your subconscious mind is like adding a visual movie to it. The affirmation covers the auditory portion of the program, but now you need to add the visual element to it. The auditory portion of the program activates your left brain, its more logical, practical side. The visual images activate the right brain, its more emotional and creative elements. So, you get the best of both sides. You must pre-visualize whatever you want to accomplish.

Willie Gault is a true warrior. He received an award for being the Best Athlete in the World in 1991. He was considered the fastest man in football. He was also considered the second fastest man in the world, next to Carl Lewis. He won Gold Medals in the Summer and Winter Olympics.

One of the best practices is to make it a short mental movie. Break it down to a short, visual active scene. Focus on your priority goal but in a total visual state and scene. It doesn't matter what your goal is; it could be making more money, being more successful, having a better relationship, facing a fear, or becoming a stronger and better fighter. The same approach can be used for any goal or accomplishment. The more real you can make the scene in your mind visually, the stronger the chance that your subconscious mind will accept, digest and activate it. The best way to make the scene more real is to add all the real sensations to it. Activate all of your senses, visual, sound, smell, touch, and color. For example, let's say you want to win a fight against a specific fighter. Visualize and see yourself mentally in the arena, dojo, ring, or exact place you are going to fight. See the colors of that facility. Smell the air. What does it smell like? Hear the sounds going on around you. What will they be? Feel the air and the atmosphere. Feel yourself putting your gi or fighting attire on. What do your feet feel like on the ground or floor that you are going to fight on? While you are doing all of this, visualize yourself acquiring the proper warrior state of mind, optimum peak performance mental state or whatever state is best for the situation you are in. Then add one of the most important elements of all, which could be equal to having a turbo-charger: the proper emotional mental and physical state. Create the emotional state you would have after you just won a championship fight, acquired a huge amount of money, got an incredible raise or promotion, or became totally successful in your career! You need that to add extra energy and excitement to your visualization.

Then see yourself accomplish exactly what you want, without any fears, doubts or insecurities. The more focused, concentrated and real you can make the imagery, the more powerful it will become. You will make your subconscious mind completely believe your imagery is already reality and that portion of your brain will do everything in its power to make it happen. The more you practice and see it happening mentally, the more focused it will become. Practice it at least once a day for awhile, but amp it up to three, four or as many times as possible a day.

Many people are familiar with one of the original tests, executed to prove the value of imagery and visualization to an activity or sport. There were three test groups of students that took part in a mental programming experiment based on shooting a basketball. Before the test, all the participating students shooting abilities were tested and reported. Group One was told, "Don't play basketball for a month. In fact, just forget about basketball for the entire month." Group Two was told, "You are each to practice shooting baskets for one full hour a day, everyday of the month." Group Three was told, "You are to spend one hour imagining you are successfully shooting baskets. Visualize every detail of your accomplishments in your mind, but don't physically shoot any baskets." The three groups were tested again on their basketball shooting ability one month later. Group One, which hadn't played for a month, tested the same as they did the first time. Group Two, which had practiced a full hour a day for a month, demonstrated a 24 percent improvement. Group Three, which had only imagined they were successfully shooting baskets for an hour a day, tested and displayed a 23 percent improvement, only one percentage point less than the group that was actually practicing shooting baskets.

The two best times to practice your visualizations are just before you go to sleep at night and just when you wake up in the morning. After you stretch out and calm down from the day, your mind will automatically start going into an alpha mental state. Then right after you wake up in the morning, your mind will tune back into that alpha state. Lie there a few more minutes and go through your mental movie and positive auditory statements.

Here's another advantage. After practicing your imagery just before you go to sleep, your subconscious mind, being in the alpha state, will start to accept the information you are programming and your subconscious mind will digest and work on it all night. Then, in the morning, you will remind yourself again of your visual positive movie and affirmations to carry throughout the day. Just before you are about to perform, compete, fight, meet with your boss or actually do what you are attempting to achieve, you should do one final intense, concentrated perfect mental rehearsal. This way it will be imbedded deeply in your mind. This will help your mind and body to be totally focused on your goal, without any distractions—internally or externally.

Try not to make all of your visualizations too general or broad. It is great to see yourself very successful and rich, but it is better to visualize and concentrate the imagery on the specific goals that will help you to get there. You must have a balance between the big general goals and the specific ones, as mentioned earlier.

There are four different types of basic focuses you should be aware of and concentrate on. The first is broad and external, taking in the full outer picture. This would be like walking into a huge auditorium where you are going to perform or fight, as you take in and digest that surrounding atmosphere and start to integrate it with your performance. The second is broad internal focusing. This is how you are going to focus your basic personal performance in this environment or facility. Third is narrow external focus. This is directing attention outwardly on your personal external action itself. The fourth or final focus is narrow internal. This is the pinpointed focus you acquire by going deep within yourself mentally and physically. You make sure you are centered, focused and your mind and body are one.

It is also good to concentrate your imagery on what you see as your hardest challenges or obstacles. It is important not to forget to concentrate on your mental goals, too. If you have materialized incredibly strong focused visualizations, but have a fear, insecurity or phobia about having success, more money or being a great fighter, you will sabotage yourself quickly.

The most potent practice of your visualization is to imagine, think and act as if you have already accomplished the goal you had in your mind. You must get your subconscious mind to completely believe you have already achieved your goal. You must also convince your conscious mind you have also already attained it, too. It is also good to thank God, heaven, the universe or whatever your spiritual belief is for assisting you in attaining your goal or new level.

It has been scientifically proven that when you visualize an activity or performance at a deep level in your mind you achieve small muscular fiber impulses, which duplicate the activity you are going to perform at a more perfect level. Remember this principle: the future has already happened, because it has already happened in your mind. We all have very powerful creative abilities imbedded deep in our minds. We have the ability to create beyond limits. You are the only one who can place limits on what you want to create yourself to be. Some of the top achievers and athletes have mastered these concepts and principles when they were young, and it paid off. Willie Gault is one of these unique individuals. In one of our earlier personal talks, years ago, he said something that impressed me. He mentioned when he was six or seven years old he already had a vision and goal that he wanted to be an incredible football player and the best that he could be. He said, "I pictured and visualized it daily in my mind, even as kid." It is obvious from the record that he achieved that. He confided in me, that he practiced everything we discussed in this chapter, as did the majority of successful athletes and achievers.

Chapter 13

Optimum Peak Performance Mental States

Your inner state of mind should be like a great calm sea. Look at your opponent and your life like you are gazing at a mountain in the distance. Your mind should be nowhere in particular ... until you focus. The moon has no intent to cast its shadow anywhere, nor does the pond design to dodge the moon. Never think of the attack as you release, the arrow or are ready to strike. A high-level warrior or samurai always cuts himself first before he cuts others. He first cuts, attacks or eliminates his own ego. The highest level is to fight without fighting.

You must first cut the enemy within yourself, your ego. In kyudo (Japanese archery), shooting the arrow at the target is no different than shooting at yourself. In the true warrior's mind, the opponent doesn't exist. He is merely an obstacle on his path. The conflicts you have with your opponents or enemies are only yourself reflecting back to you. In the finality of the engagement, the real fight is only against yourself. One shot, one life, one attack. Chance or opportunity. If you are not ready and don't take advantage of this opportunity, whether you created it or it came your way, you may not get another chance again, for a million years. First attack with your spirit! Use your, (ki, chi) or internal energy. Or you may have to be prepared to evade your opponent's or attacker's (ki or chi) internal energy.

When one eye is fixed on your destination, there is only one eye to find your path. Conflicts of right and wrong can cloud your mind. You must attempt to perceive things with a non-biased, open, unattached mind. To find the unclouded truth in your life, don't concern yourself with right and wrong. If you see truth in the morning, you can die in the afternoon with no regrets. If you are on the path of truth, it doesn't matter if the path is 10,000 miles long. These last two statements originate from Buddhism. Individuals have conflicts in their training and their lives, because they have contradictions in their minds. A minute difference is enough to divide heaven and earth. It is the same when you have a conflict in life or have to face an opponent. A minor element on one side or the other is enough to make a big difference. You must persevere to acquire that one minor element, which can be the difference between life and death. You can eventually conquer and control your opponent by virtue of your own mind. The person with the most choices usually has the most ways of looking at things. Great minds discuss ideas; average minds discuss events; small minds discuss people.

The majority of these statements, sound mysterious or abstract to a Western-mentality individual. Most of these views are from an Eastern philosophy and understanding. Sometimes these statements or parables will sound contradictory. Each one depicts a certain example that can be utilized to acquire a better peak performance mentality from a more Eastern understanding. It is sometimes described as being in a Zen state of mind.

What is a Zen state of mind? Zen in Japanese just means to meditate. To first acquire that Zen state of mind, you must clear your mind. Clear your mind of what? Clear it of thinking. Stop your brain from thinking and silence your mind. Don't think. If any thoughts come up, just let them go and don't build on them. Quiet and calm your mind down. Then you can start to get in more of a meditative mental state. You don't even have to close

*Greg Scott fighting at the Nisei Week Championship Tournament.
Greg has a great balance in his training. He is extremely effective
in real fights and also in karate tournament competitions.*

your eyes. Japanese, also refers to that state as mushin or "no-mind," which just means your brain is not thinking. In the West, that mental state is known as being in the zone, a peak performance mental state. They are all similar.

When they teach this mental state in the East, they are quite visual and use pictures to help explain it. To force an individual to think beyond logic, they like to talk in abstract concepts and parables. The right side of our brain sees more visually and the left side of our brain is more organized by words, logic and the rational. When your right brain sees the picture, it helps create the mental state and shuts off the left side of your brain. Thus, the statement, your inner state of mind should be like a great calm sea. When you picture this great calm sea in your mind, your mind calms down and attempts to become that.

Now, let's look at the second statement. Look at your opponent like you are gazing at a mountain in the distance. If you actually looked at a very beautiful mountain in the distance, you would naturally take in all of the scenery at once. Again your mind calms down to depict that scene. Of course, if you let it, the left side of your brain will kick in and start describing it. The first moment you gaze at it, while you are taking in everything and before you start thinking, creates that mental state. The right side of the brain sees in pictures and feels emotions. The pictures in our minds will create certain emotions. This is all the right side of the brain. It is said that the majority of men communicate through the left side of their brain and the majority of women communicate through the right. In that one statement, you can see how communication can be so misinterpreted.

If you want to really create that optimum peak performance mental state, you cannot think of yourself or your own ego. Your mind will become only attached to yourself or your ego and it cannot expand to its true capacity. That is why they talk about cutting yourself first and becoming unattached to yourself. In Buddhism, when they say right or wrong can be a disease of the mind, it only means not be too biased one way or another. If you are biased toward one point of view, your mind becomes totally attached to that point of view and you cannot see anything else from any other point of view. When you become attached to only one way, your mind becomes imprisoned and cannot express its peak potential and capacity. It will only work with the capacity of the attachments you gave it. When you are not attached to any points of view, your mind expands and has an unlimited capacity to express itself, as you decide.

Your mind may be moving freely, but if you let it, it can become attached to something just for a moment; being stuck for that moment can make the difference in a life-or-death situation. When you are in an experience and that experience makes you feel a certain way, that experience is mirroring back to you something about you and your mentality. Most people avoid looking at themselves very strictly and only get caught up in the emotion, attachment or feeling of the experience. They don't look at themselves clearly and don't learn anything new about themselves from that experience. A true warrior will. He will use the way he feels during that experience and use it like a barometer to study where he is and where he should be mentally.

The statement about different minds discussing different elements has a special meaning. A great mind with an expanded mentality doesn't get attached or caught up in small matters that don't make a difference. A great mind of an individual keeps his mind expanded and attempts to focus on the major ideas that will affect the whole human race. A person with a lesser mentality will become more attached to events that have occurred or will occur. Finally, an individual with an even smaller mentality will stay attached to what is happening with people, which doesn't help anyone. I recommend reading the first paragraph again and experiencing the mental state each statement creates in your mind as you attempt to visualize or contemplate it.

When both brain hemispheres (right and left) are synchronized, you are accomplishing the most important element in acquiring a peak performance mental state. You have to balance your logical, rational and intelligent training and information with your creative, emotional and intuitive training. Then you acquire the best of both worlds to utilize or create your ultimate peak performance activity or productive mental state. What inhibits your mental states is getting stuck or attached to elements of understanding in the left or right brain. You can really limit your think-

*Sumo wrestlers executing intense spirit while competing.
They are displaying a focused optimum
peak performance mentality.*

ing and understanding by becoming stuck and attached to just a couple of basic concepts in life. For example, let's say someone subconsciously only accepts data and information that will support his fundamental belief system. In this case, he can then become a very radical fundamentalist thinker. It will be extremely hard for him to see, understand and accept other people's points of view. This type of person is very much stuck and attached to certain elements in the left side of his brain. Remember the old saying, "Most average people only use five percent of their brain and mental capacity?" The first step in utilizing a much bigger capacity of your brain and mind is to synchronize both brain hemispheres. To that, add the various subjects discussed in this book, (visualizing, attitude, non-attachment.)

So, how do you tap into and utilize a fuller capacity of the right and left side of your brain at the same time? It is very simple, through a specific breathing technique. This will be discussed further and to a greater extent in a later chapter, but we'll start with one breathing technique here. You first calm your mind. Start breathing in your lower abdomen, building the energy there, like it was a small powerful energy center. Keep your mouth closed, put your tongue on the top of your palate in your mouth and only exhale through the nose. Your eyes can be open or closed, depending on what your focus and goal are. Visualize yourself exhaling your breath from your lower abdomen and up through your nose, but hold the air back a bit in the back of your throat. Make it sound like a hissing, coming from the back of your throat. Imagine that hissing sound is like a teapot building up steam and exhaling it, however you want. You can make the hissing very soft and light or very strong and intense. That will intensify the energy. Keep your mind clear and focused on whatever goal, activity or mental state you want to enhance. This one breathing technique will automatically synchronize both hemispheres, which will tap you into a much bigger capacity mental state.

There are many degrees and levels of an optimum peak performance mental state. It depends how concentrated and focused you can become. It also depends on how completely you can synchronize your mental state with your physical and technical abilities, so they all work as one efficient unit. There are so many distractions that can pull you away from that concentration state ... even for a moment. As mentioned, when two high-level warriors face each other in a fight, it is not just a question of who is technically better. It is more, who losses concentration and focus just for a split second. Then one warrior will take advantage of that gap and capitalize on it to destroy his opponent. That is all it takes sometimes. Michael Jordan, Muhammad Ali, Wayne Gretzky, Tiger Woods, Andre Agassi and numerous others all have their own way of acquiring their peak performance mental state before they perform. Some can explain it and others can't. They have just been doing it so long that the process becomes subconscious and automatic. Everyone has to learn his own particular process, adhering to the basic effective concepts discussed here.

The warrior peak performance mental state is the same thing, except a warrior has a bigger element, to keep from distracting him. It's called death. In battle, if a warrior starts worrying about not getting hurt, shot or killed, it will get him out of that peak performance mental state so fast that it will be very difficult to recover ... and he probably won't. Nothing is wrong with feeling fear, but it has to be controlled and it has to work for you.

I have seen many top warriors and fighters display incredible focus and concentration through the years. Don DePree is one of the top karate warriors and realistic fighters in modern times, with a natural killer instinct. I've seen him fight numerous times and destroy many opponents. Our karate teacher, Tsutomu Ohshima, once called Don out. He was to face an extremely tough and mentally strong opponent for a very important event. I was sitting next to him on the floor when that happened. When his name was called, he took off his necklace, turned to look at me and give me the necklace. When I looked straight in his eyes, the hair on the back of my neck stood up. His eyes were like laser beams, and he looked right through me like I wasn't there. I felt like he had thrown his life away with no fear of dying, but he would fight until he died. I immediately knew his opponent would have no idea what he was about to face and that was proved true, after the first engagement. That was an ideal optimum peak performance mental state, at the highest level.

One of the smartest fighters I have ever seen, who quickly and automatically expressed one of the fastest ultimate peak performance mental states, is a man named Greg Scott. He is also a fifth-degree black belt with Tsutomu Ohshima and has trained and dedicated his entire life to karate. He is an average sized individual, but one of the best I've ever seen with a special ability to

switch immediately into the warrior mentality and peak performance mental state. Through the years, I have seen him face some
of the best technical and most ferocious fighters around and he
always is able to beat them. He calculates an opponent faster
than anyone I have ever seen and is able to not only use his
opponent's weaknesses against him, but also his strengths. If an
opponent has an incredible favorite technique, Greg gets him to
execute it under his conditions and not his opponent's conditions. Then he doesn't have to be concerned about his opponent's best and favorite technique. He is an expert at expressing
his fullness to his opponent's emptiness.

Chapter 14

Combat Mentality

The combat mentality is also an optimum peak performance mental state, but takes it to another major level. The combat mentality is a mental peak performance state, applied to real combat. There are numerous types of combat, but in real combat, there is one common denominator. It is life or death.

A sports performance athlete can be distracted mentally by numerous elements, but in most cases, it will not be death. There are some sports and competitions that are very risky and an individual can get killed, but it is rare. In combat and on the battlefield, whether it's one-on-one or armies facing armies, death is constantly staring you down. That will get an individual distracted very quickly. If one isn't prepared for that, it will greatly influence how he will ultimately perform and determine whether he will survive or perish.

What is the most important element that can help a warrior to survive in combat or battle? Spirit! A true warrior must have a fearless spirit against all odds. It doesn't mean he doesn't fear anything, but he knows how to control and redirect fear to be more effective in surviving and dominating his opponent. Death is usually the wild card worrying most human beings, unless they have trained themselves to face it with the appropriate mentality. Most individuals can be pretty brave and attempt a lot of things, but would have second thoughts, if they knew that they had a strong chance of dying. Some extreme sports can be dangerous, but most athletes don't really think they will die until it is too late.

How do the various military groups train their soldiers to face this ever present psychological threat? They have to deal with this factor all the time. The ones that have the most success with training soldiers on how to deal with facing death or grave bodily harm are the elite forces, such as Delta Force, Special Forces, Navy Seals, Rangers and Force Recon Marines. Other countries have their own elite forces that also train to deal with that same element. They train these elite soldiers so much on every level that they function—mentally, physically, tactically and technically—automatically. They can't afford to start thinking how awful an experience will be and get stuck in their negative emotions. If they did, their mind will become so encompassed with worry and concern for themselves that they wouldn't be able to complete their mission successfully. Automatic responses reduce the likelihood of stupid or careless mistakes. They are all so highly trained mentally, physically, tactically, strategically and technically to operate in and under any conditions that their training will carry them through most situations. They train eight to twelve hours a day in all aspects, various schools and conditions—sometimes for years—before they are put into a real mission. The training of these elite soldiers is so realistic that when they are in a real mission, they have already performed it hundreds of times. They have passed all limits in their training, so they have acquired an unlimited mentality. You can put them in almost any combat or survival situations and somehow they will calculate how to survive. If there is a chance that they don't, they will go down like warriors. There is nothing in between for these types incredibly trained elite soldiers. If they do get hit, injured or shot, they will deal with that if and when it happens, like a warrior, without emotional attachment before or in the event.

Besides exhaustive training, a warrior doesn't get to this level, unless he has developed a deep fortified character and integrity.

*Ken Osborne, one of Tsutomu Ohshima's top senior black belts.
He has trained and taught karate over 45 years. Ken is considered
one of the best foot-sweepers in the world.*

Like that old saying, "They have been baptized in fire and blood and come out steel!" Through their intense training, they have developed a deep professionalism and pride into who they are, what their mission is, and what they do, represent and stand for. This pride and professionalism helps to temper their warrior spirit and what they represent to all people. When it comes down to it, it is the warrior or soldier that really fights for democracy and freedom of consciousness in this world. They are the ones who have the spirit, strength and fortitude to make a difference for everyone else. Their sacrifice has assisted the human race to evolve ... mentally, spiritually, physically and technically.

Many of these ancient concepts are taken from the Japanese samurai warriors. Japan was in a feudal period for more than a thousand years, and the samurai had time to evolve their fight-

Tom Muzila and Ken Osborne climbing near the top of Mt. Shasta in Northern California.

ing spirit, mentality and technique to a top level. They discovered what worked and was most effective in battle and combat ... mentally, physically and technically.

They had many sayings that were actually fighting concepts and principles. "Under the sword is hell, but beyond the sword is heaven." If your opponent had a sword over your head and was ready to attack and you stayed there or tried to block it, which was hell. If your opponent had the sword over your head and was ready to attack, but you attacked first by going straight into his attack and sword at the precise moment and ended up behind him after he struck, that was heaven. Of course, it takes some mental strength and courage to be able to do that, and that's what the higher-level samurai attempted to do.

This same concept can be applied to many situations and experiences in life, even though we are talking about a sword confrontation here. Following is another concept. You are attacking your enemy with a sword. At the same moment your enemy makes a strike and cuts your legs off while you are attacking, you should still be attacking with full spirit, energy and commitment. So much, in fact, that your forward momentum enables you to move in and kill your opponent. This state is very hard for most people to comprehend. Your commitment and spirit is so phenomenally strong, that even with your legs cut off, you still continue your attack and destroy your opponent.

"If your opponent bites you, jump in his mouth and a whole new world will open up." This means that when your adversary attacks you, whether he hits you or cuts you, attack his attack even more powerfully. Most individuals run away from a strong attack. A true warrior would attack his opponent's attack with ferocity to completely destroy his opponent.

Closely related: "If your opponent cuts your skin, take a piece of his muscle." Whatever your opponent does to you, do more damage to him, because you are continually attacking him with your strong spirit, no matter what happens to you. Your spirit is so strong that—even if an opponent hits you—you come back and knock him out. If he cuts you on the arm with his sword, come back with your stroke and kill him. To accomplish this, you first must have the correct mind-set. Most people engaged in this type of conflict would be completely shocked if they got cut, hit or wounded. They would not be able to continue. Their mind would be consumed with their injury.

How can a samurai or warrior be able to accomplish these tasks under these types of conditions? This is the secret. Some individuals will talk about it, but it is extremely hard to actually do it. You cannot fake it. There is only one way and that is to actually do it and experience it. A true samurai's first mission is to face death and train his mind to accept it, surrender to it and pass through fears. When a warrior actually trains himself to do that, he has passed through a gateway that very few have entered.

"If a samurai or warrior has a choice of an action in combat that could cause life or death, he will always pick death." For a logical, rational person, this sounds contradictory. Why would a person pick death? It does go against all logic and human nature. Only an extremely well-trained warrior would understand. If he picked an action in combat, which meant he could die, he would subconsciously choose that. He believed, if his survival was heaven's will, aligned with his consciousness than he would survive. By picking death and surviving, he would have achieved an enlightenment of not being attached to death. He would be able to completely express his true potential and not be inhibited or concerned about dying in battle. Under these conditions, he would be able to express an unlimited freedom and heightened liberation in battle. He believed, after he had reached this mental state in battle a couple of times, he could express his highest potential in fighting. It doesn't matter what type of fighting—whether hand-to-hand, knives, guns, clubs or military assault rifles. When a warrior has this type of mentality, he can make a decision to accept death without hesitation at any moment. When a warrior faces death, he immediately decides to face, attack, and penetrate it. If he survives, he will pass through that experience with a new and heightened mentality.

The Japanese samurai have a special word, kokoro. Their definition sounds like two contradictory elements, but it reveals the appropriate mentality of a true warrior. It combines the ability to throw your life away without any regrets, but at the same time not surrendering your life and fighting continuously to the last precious moment that your body holds life. The samurai believe that if a warrior can express this unlimited mental potential, he has the recipe to create miracles in battle.

A warrior always trains for the unexpected. So, when the unexpected happens, he is ready. A normal person is only ready and programmed for the expected. He is usually useless in the face of the unexpected. A true warrior makes his personal training as hard, as if not harder than a real situation. Therefore, when a real situation happens, he may even be over trained and ready for it. If a warrior survives the first couple of moments of an encounter, he knows he has to depend upon his well-trained skill to survive the next few moments. If he survives those early moments, he also knows he can possibly survive this situation.

A warrior will prepare for every encounter as if it were his last or an encounter to the death. He cannot let his concentration lapse for even a split second, as that split second can mean life or death. How many individuals have this warrior spirit? Of course, an individual can train to a certain extent to become a warrior, but very few, naturally have this spirit. There may be only one of 100 men, but that means only one that will actually fight. There may be only one of a couple hundred thousand that is a true warrior. He has the special ability to kill many people in battle, as well as to save many people, too.

Yasunori Ono, who is from Japan. He is one of Tsutomu Ohshima's top black belt fighters in Japan. He is also considered one of the top karate men in the world. He looks very unassuming here, but can be very deadly.

Besides extreme and focused training, what else can a warrior do to get himself to this level of perfection in battle, especially when he has to face death? There is one more important element, and it is the main secret to accomplish this. This practice is very much tied into many of the elements and aspects already discussed. It is the mental element, but it involves taking it to the optimum levels. Again, it is hard for people who haven't trained in these warrior concepts to understand these principles, because they do seem to go against all human nature. That is why it is important to train so hard mentally, physically and technically to penetrate these natural human instincts.

The hardest human instinct to face is the one to stay alive at all costs. This is the most primitive human survival instinct. In the

Lamon Brewster held the WBO World Heavyweight Boxing Championship. He has defended his title many times with the mentality and spirit of a true warrior.

true warrior's world, this is the final element to face and detach himself from. This is not to be confused with ordinary fears, phobias and profound insecurities. There are so many people who have these fears and they worry about them happening to them everyday of their life. They are so totally consumed with them that they start to govern their lives. What they should do? What type of profession? Where they should go on trips? Who they should get to know or become friends with? The irony in this is that many of these types of people end up being confronted and actually dying by the element they fear the most. This could be a person who has a grave fear of falling, drowning, getting burned or shot. They actually end up dying in the way they fear the most. "Whatever you think about most expands." It's almost as if your subconscious mind is attracted to face what you fear most and are mentally attached to, but your conscious mind doesn't have the right mentality to face and get through it.

The warrior or high-level samurai has a different approach to dealing with the natural instinct to stay alive. Yet this approach allows him to live more advantageously. He will meditate on every way possible he could die until he has totally accepted, surrendered and become unattached to it. He will imagine it so vividly and strongly that in his mind the real situation is happening. The fearful person discussed earlier would get stuck mentally on all the ways he could avoid the situation. But there are no ways to avoid it, because he cannot escape from his own mind. On the other hand, the warrior imagines it so much that he eventually accepts it, but he isn't mentally attached to it. He actually experiences his own death in his mind and realizes that it is not important. This is because he has faced it and lived it many times in his mind; to him he has already faced a real experience and understands that it is an inevitable part of existence. It is similar to an individual practicing karate who is petrified of getting hit in the face. After he has been hit in the face a couple of times with the right mentality, he realizes that it is not such a big deal and gets over it. He doesn't give it too much attention or emotional energy. The event or experience in your mind is relative.

This is similar to the warrior who imagines and experiences every possible way he could die in his mind. He doesn't expend too much energy after he has faced and accepted all those possibilities in his mind. Eventually, if the warrior ends up facing a similar situation in reality, which he has faced and accepted in his mind for many years, he is ready for it. It is not sometime new or shocking to his mind. Now he can express himself in combat without any attachments or reluctance to inhibit his performance. This is the secret of becoming a warrior.

We spoke about Miyamoto Musashi earlier. As we mentioned, he was considered one of the best swordsmen in history. He was also the most notable and famous. There were a few who were also great top swordsmen at the time, but they were not as notable or famous. One was Mariya Enshiro; he lived from 1660 to 1743. He was the third generation descendent from Harigaya Sekuin, discussed earlier. He introduced and made popular the sword "Gates of Heaven" practice. Miyamoto Musashi had fewer than 100 duels during his life. Mariya Enshiro fought 1,000 duels throughout his entire life. He accepted all challenges from opponents using all kinds of weapons, such as bokken, shinai, jo, kon (long bo), sword, spear or kama. Whatever weapons his opponent selected, Mariya used only an oak bokken (wooden sword) and still beat them. Mariya was a master of the sword, "Gates of Heaven" practice. He was reported as saying, "He could see his opponent's movements three days ahead of time." His level was described as "Watermoon Devil." This means that there is no gap between the time the moon moves over the water and the time it takes for a reflection to appear.

One not well known is Yasunori Ono. He is one of Tsutomu Ohshima's top black belts in the world. He not only dominated the majority of all karate tournaments in Japan for many years, but he also always applied his fighting ability to a real fight with no rules. He has an unorthodox style, but it is effective and realistic. He can instantly switch his fighting style from karate tournament with rules to a life-and-death fight. His tactics and strategies are phenomenal. He is also an expert strategist. There was a time, he decided to fight in a major tournament in Japan and found out who was the toughest opponent. He had heard of him and knew his opponent had a powerful front kick and had beaten everyone in various conditions. He has also broken a number of his opponent's ribs with it too, so it was very effective. One of Yasunori Ono's favorite techniques was to attack first instinctively and explosively with a front jab (maite), which was one of the best in the country. He felt he could beat this opponent with the strong front kick, but he was concerned he would get disqualified and lose the tournament. He changed his strategy and started working on a basic down block (gedan barai) on a heavy bag

Fred House working with K-9's at the Utah State Penitentiary.
He was killed in the line of duty. He received the Medal of Valor
from the state of Utah, for his brave actions.

and applying it to this specific opponent and situation. The day
the tournament came, Ono ended up facing that opponent with
the fast and powerful front kick. Ono blocked the kick and broke
his opponent's leg. As a result, he couldn't continue and Ono
won the tournament. This may seem cruel to some people, but
it is a part of fighting..

In the late 1960s, one of the black belts brought an oak
board to our Los Angeles dojo. A few of the senior black belts
there thought they would try to break it. Breaking pine boards,
even up to six of them with a side-thrust kick is not so difficult.
This was a very hard and thick oak board. Many of the black belts
tried it and failed. They couldn't do anything with it. They tried
elbows and kicks and the board wouldn't give at all. Ono was
there and was watching the whole thing. Eventually, he tried

Law Enforcement Training Center in Utah, named in honor of Fred House.

breaking it too. He had a number of black belts hold it for him. When he would kick it, he would end up driving the four black belts backward and still the board wouldn't give at all. They put the board down and everyone stayed there a little longer and forgot about the board. They took it for granted that it couldn't be broken. A few of the black belts noticed Ono was pacing back and forth and looked like he was in a very concentrated mental state. About 10 minutes later, he walked over to the board and leaned it up against a solid wooden step at a 45-degree angle. He stepped on it with a stomping kick (fumikomi). The board not only broke, but it exploded into a number of pieces.

One of the truest warriors I've ever seen is a man named Ken Osborne. I've seen him face some of the toughest karate practitioners on the planet.

He has no fear of death or dying. He was originally Chuck Norris's first black belt and later started training with Tsutomu Ohshima. Ken started training in the early 1960s. Through the years, anytime I have suggested any marathon karate practices to him, he always jumped in without hesitating ... or knowing anything about it. Still, he always accomplished it. He is a unique warrior who would face any opponent, anytime, anywhere and under any conditions. When I have suggested that he and I execute 10,000 front kicks, without any hesitation, he would say, "OK." When I said to him, "Let's climb Mt. Shasta in half of a day," he said, "OK." He was always ready to face death at anytime.

Another unique individual is Guy Trimble. I have known Guy for more than 35 years. He has trained extensively in Shotokan karate the entire time. Guy has made an extensive study into the effective application of techniques in kata (forms) in karate. He has been at this for more than 20 years. His practices and research methods invite comparison to a biologist or archeologist at work. He first attempts to imagine how it was in an actual battle hundreds of years ago. He studies the kata, the techniques and all of their possible applications. Through the years, he actually has had opponents attack him in various realistic ways with weapons, including swords, clubs, knives, etc. He actually uses sharp and dangerous weapons, and he has made all kinds of equipment to train with and apply in and against realistic attacks. He attempts to find which techniques work and are effective and realistic with live attacks and live weapons. If an application or technique isn't effective under a live attack or realistic situation, he discards it. Guy really attempts to apply a technique in a live situation to see if it actually could work. There are very few who go to this extent to apply techniques under very realistic situations and with real weapons. Guy has the combat warrior mentality.

There are many unique warriors I have met and had the opportunity to train with through the years. I'm sorry there isn't space to include all of them in this book. One of the toughest warriors I knew very well was a man named Fred House. Fred had two brothers, Tom and Gary. Like their brother, both Tom and Gary were strong mentally and always pushed themselves beyond limits. Fred worked for the Utah State Prison system for many years. When there were fights, challenges, breakouts or riots, he was the first one who volunteered to defuse them and he did it in his own special way. He would take on all challenges from the prisoners, until they wouldn't challenge him any more.

He utilized all of these as opportunities to test his karate techniques and tactics. Fred had a very dangerous reputation with the prisoners. One day a riot broke out in one wing of the prison. There were about 30 prisoners who broke out rioting and were causing total chaos. The prison anti-riot squad was there in a line with shields, helmets and clubs. Fred got there with no protective gear on, stepped out in front of the line of guards and ordered them to stand down. The prisoners yelled back, cussing and saying they were going to kill him. Fred's classic line and response was, "Come on! You can make it! Be somebody!" Of course, none of the prisoners came to challenge him.

Unfortunately, Fred was killed in the line of duty in 1988 in Marion, Utah. A polygamist was held up in a cabin with a few other men, women and children. He already had many crimes against him. He declared his cabin and property a separate country. There were more than 150 law enforcement officers there, including the FBI, state troopers, police and sheriffs. Everyone was trying to get him to surrender. Of course, the polygamist and his supporters weren't having anything to do with surrendering.

The siege lasted 13 days. Fred was an expert with K-9 units or police dogs and proposed a plan to the FBI. They liked his plan and decided to let Fred and his dog sneak up close to the cabin to attempt to be the first one to subdue the polygamist and initiate the assault. Fred was the first one in with his dog and was shot by a sniper in the cabin. Of course, the assault was successful, but it was at the sacrifice of Fred's life.

There have been some outstanding professional boxers throughout history, such as Mohammad Ali, Sugar Ray Robinson, Sugar Ray Leonard, and Mike Tyson. A few have a natural killer instinct. Some have tremendous physical genetic abilities and are phenomenally trained on top of that. Others have a fantastic level of self-confidence. Very few have a good balance of all these attributes. These elements should be balanced first in one's mentality and then in one's practice with mental, physical, tactical, and consciousness training.

One unique boxer I've known and worked with, I believe has acquired a sound balance of these warrior qualities, is Lamon Brewster. He is presently the WBO World heavyweight championship boxer. He also has the North American belt and has had more than 32 professional fights. Lamon is one of the humblest boxers, yet he has the heart and mentality to be one of the most furious. He has proven this in the ring. He has been considered the underdog a few times and won. He stays humble, although his capacity gets better and stronger.

This is a tough balance to hold in your mind. You have to be able to turn the switch on and off—and also to specific degrees—to keep an appropriate balance for the situation you're in. Lamon has learned to do this through his strict mental, physical and spiritual training. His secret isn't just to train hard to learn how to beat big, strong and well-trained opponents. His secret is to face himself mentally, physically and spiritually on every level. He has faced all of his fears, mental blocks and insecurities. Along with becoming a world champion heavyweight boxer, he also wanted to become the best quality human being he could. He did everything he could to develop a limitless mentality. Then he was able to face big, powerful well-trained opponents who were 6 feet 4, seven inches taller than he.

Chapter 15

High-Powered Breathing Techniques for Inner Power

Breathing is our main life force. We can stay alive for weeks or even months without food. We can even stay alive without water for seven to 14 days. Without air or breathing, we can only make it a few minutes. Some yogi sects from India have an interesting philosophy related to breath, and it is very different from the Western approach of having a healthy life.

Westerners tend to consider good healthy food, exercise and limited stress as keys to increasing health and longevity. These are all important, but the yogi approach puts an emphasis on breathing. They estimate that we have about 60,000,000 total breaths in our life. The faster we use them and the more unhealthy or shallow the breaths are, the more it will decrease and lessen our life span. If we expand and us our breaths more efficiently, it can increase our health and expand our life time. If a person uses those breaths in 40, 50 or 60 years, that is when he will die or pass away. So, why would a person use those breaths up fast?

The yogis have another saying. They say that an average person breathes about 16 times per minute. An expert in an art such as yoga, karate or dance breathes about eight times per minute.

A master who has been practicing a specific art and dedicated his life to it would breathe about four times per minute. Fewer breaths each minute would extend those 60,000,000 breaths for many years.

There is another understanding related to the quality of breaths that goes along with this. When a person is under a huge amount of stress, he will breathe mainly in his upper lungs. He will also execute much shorter and shallower breaths. The air will not be able to get deep down and circulate in the lower lungs, and that isn't healthy. If an individual breathes in this manner and has a stressful lifestyle, he will surely use those breaths much quicker. He would also be executing shallow, unhealthy breaths. In karate and the martial arts, this is known as having too much power in one's shoulders.

These unhealthy breaths would eventually have an effect on most of the other major organs in the body. Through the years, this effect would compound and create problems and all kinds of other diseases, too. This understanding ties into another concept, related to the quality of breath and the consciousness of one's mentality. The higher-level yogis and martial artists say that a stressful person breathes in his shoulders. An average person breathes in his upper lungs. An expert or well-trained person breathes in his lower abdomen, longer breaths, deeper and healthier.

They also have another interesting concept, which sounds very esoteric, but it does have meaning, if you perceive it from the appropriate mentality. One who really speaks truth breathes from his feet. Of course, air doesn't really go there, but it could be a connection of breathing to the ground and also acquiring energy from there. This sense suggests a oneness with nature and the universe. When a person is stressed out and breathes more in his shoulders (again air doesn't go there), he has more of a conscious connection with his shoulders. This isn't good, because such a person will also become very tense and tight in his shoulders. This added extra stress or power in the shoulders disconnects the whole body. It is very hard to make the body move as one unit in this state. In the martial arts, some would say he has too much conscious power in his shoulders, which isn't necessary. This conscious tension and power in the shoulders also creates more stress and tension in the mind. If an individual practices longer, deeper breathing focused from the lower abdomen but acquires a sense of connection with his feet to the ground and nature, he will be breathing much more effectively and efficiently. This will allow his state of mind, to be much calmer. This breathing would help create and keep a much

Tom Muzila is teaching internal (ki or chi) breathing exercises to Victoria Plarr, Miss World Galaxy.

less stressful life and healthy organs and body. When you add a healthy diet and appropriate training and exercise, it can all add up to greater longevity.

Breathing is the real secret to connecting your mind and body. If you want to be able to perform or execute any skill, ability or art, your mind and body have to work and move as one unit, synchronized perfectly together. This is evident in sports, arts, martial arts and music. Breathing, synchronized with body movement and the proper rhythm and pacing, will create a more perfect, effective, efficient, powerful movement. This could be a painting brush stroke or a martial arts attack. You have to practice and train, so you have a strong sense and focus that your breathing is going with your movement. It is best to imagine that breath or energy is traveling through your arms, fingers or palms with the movement you are executing. When you are pushing a car or lifting a weight, you don't breath in. You breathe out or exhale with the push. You can also focus that breath or energy through your eyes, feet, legs or mind. You can imagine that breath and energy directed to any vital organ that needs to be healed. Animals and mammals do this naturally, but humans have to practice it diligently to be effective. If a dog or cat is lying next to you and you lightly push or lean on it, it will naturally exhale to counter that resistance. People have a conscious mind and can think, overreact and have too much personal emotion attached to movement. This can take away power, effectiveness and efficiency from the movement.

Breathing is also the connection between your conscious and subconscious mind. As mentioned in a previous chapter, your conscious mind is like the tip of the iceberg and your subconscious mind is the huge portion of the iceberg is under the ocean. The portion of the ice under the ocean can be 10 times larger than the portion above water. This also relates back to that common saying that average people only use only five or 10 percent of their brain capacity. It is very similar with your conscious and subconscious mind. It is very easy to change your ideas in your conscious mind, but it is very hard to change what you have experienced or filed deeply in your subconscious mind. You can attempt to talk yourself into almost anything in your conscious mind, but that doesn't mean your subconscious mind will accept it. The key and secret to getting your subconscious mind to accept a statement, belief, concept or affirmation is appropriate breathing. This is the breathing that will calm you down and prevent your conscious mind from talking too much. The beta state of mind, which is a more conscious state, was discussed in a previous chapter. You want to create an alpha state of mind, a calmer and more relaxed state. By calming your breathing, making it longer and deeper, without consciously thinking, you will create that alpha state.

Now, you can implant suggestions, concepts, beliefs and affirmations into your subconscious mind. It is very simple to do, but the majority of people will not do it often, because they are too attached to being busy, getting things done and being in a beta state of mind. It feels unproductive for most people to take the time to get in an alpha state, because they have to take the time to go within. Of course, as mentioned earlier, listening to calming music or watching peaceful, beautiful scenery can easily put you in that alpha state. When you get up, start walking around and using your mind to think, you are immediately back in that beta state.

Your breathing can be focused sharply, precisely and explosively, as in a kiai, which is called a spirit shout in karate. You focus all of your energy at one point at the precise moment you execute a strike or an attack. This explosive breathing will enhance the penetration power of your technique. When you also yell sharply at this same moment, this makes your breathing explode along with the sound. Again, this kiai has to be exactly coordinated with your technique. This includes timing, distance and alignment with the proper body state and mentality. Timed properly, breathing, kiai, timing, distance, alignment, body state, technique and your mental state can tremendously increase the power of your strike or attack. This is known as an external yell or kiai.

You can also execute an internal kiai. You do almost everything the same, except the sound is not emitted externally, but internally. This technique isn't only used in karate or martial arts. Weightlifters and powerlifters use it to increase their maximum and explosive strength. You can use coordinated breathing for many other things, too. Bruce Lee had a unique way to increase his energy and power to add to his spirit. He would actually exe-

*Tom Muzila's pit bull, whose name was Algonquin,
was born with great natural fighting spirit.*

cute a rhythmic breathing with his movement in an external continuous kiai. Most martial artist would do the opposite. It worked very well for him.

Yoga schools teach that breathing through the right nostril, stimulates the left or rational side of your brain. They also believe that when you breathe more through the left nostril it stimulates your right or intuitive-creative brain functions. So, each nostril stimulates the opposite sides of your brain. They also say that the left brain governs more the right side of the body and the right brain governs more the left side. They say that this is one reason more people are right-handed, because most people are taught to be left-brain dominant. Of course, there are people who are ambidextrous who can use both sides of their bodies with the same skill level and ability. They feel these people use both sides of their brains equally. They also believe that the right eye emanates more energy from the left brain and the left eye emanates more energy from the right brain. This is possibly why some people's right eyes are a little bigger than their left. In a way, you could almost say that some people maybe seeing, perceiving and interpreting information through the left or more logical brain.

You will notice that your breathing changes through the day. Sometimes you are breathing more through your left nostril and sometimes more through your right nostril. Some yogis believe that this is a natural phenomenon governed by your subconscious mind to balance both brain hemispheres. Your breathing usually changes from right to left nostril and visa versa every two and one-half hours. Hypothetically, the best time to make an important decision or solve a problem would be when you are breathing equally through both nostrils. In this case, you would be using both brain hemispheres in a balanced, centered way. You would combine your logical, rational brain with your emotional, creative and intuitive brain to make a decision or solve an important problem.

In yoga, to stimulate the right brain, block the right nostril and only take long deep breaths through the left nostril. Similarly, to engage the left side of the brain, block the left nostril with the thumb and take long deep breaths through the right nostril. They also practice alternate-side breathing, blocking the right nostril, breathing in through the left then blocking the left nostril and exhaling only through the right, and later reversing the direction of flow.

There are numerous views on breathing techniques and rhythms. Each discipline or art has its own. Many overlap each other. Breathing is the secret to changing your state of mind and body. If you get stressed, long deep breathing will help you to relax and get into a calmer state of mind. If you are not in a calm state of mind, it is usually not worth trying to make an important decision or solve a problem.

There are many schools of yoga and they all emphasize proper breathing techniques. Kundalini yoga has a wide variety of techniques. The major emphasis is specific breathing techniques channeled through a given posture. Many techniques employ chanting in sound-currents which combine to form mantras. These sound currents and mantras force your breathing to into a certain rhythm, similar to what Bruce Lee was doing.

Another breathing technique in kundalini yoga is called "breath of fire." You adopt a specific body posture and execute a breathing technique only through your nose, which sounds like a person hyperventilating. Execute short, strong inhales and exhales equally through your nose. This rhythm creates strong energy and heat in your body. You can also focus it mentally, so you can get anything you want in your body or mind. Yogis would go out in a snowstorm—wearing only a loincloth—dig an ice cave, crawl inside and execute breath of fire all night to stay warm and alive. That is how powerful this one breathing technique is.

An example of rhythmic breathing is the 1-4-2 concept. This is a good breathing rhythm for basic energy and balancing your body and mind. When you breathe in, count it as one count. Hold it for four counts and take two counts to exhale. You can slowly expand this, as your capacity increases. For example, you can do: 5-20-10 counts. Breath in five counts, hold it for 20 counts and exhale for 10 counts. One emphasis is to expand and hold your breathing as long as possible to increase lung capacity and the other is to exhale and hold your breath out for as long as possible. They are both extremely beneficial for increasing your breath expansion and contraction capabilities. You can change this rhythm or ratio to 5-10-10-10. The one added is the number of counts you hold your breath after the exhale. Breathe in five counts, hold 10 counts, exhale 10 counts and hold your breath out for 10 counts. When you hold your breath out longer, you increase the economy of your body working very efficiently with little air or oxygen. This technique also stimulates more activity in your brain cells.

Yogis would bury themselves under ground and use their mind, bodies and breathing the most efficient way so they could last a long time with hardly any energy, air or oxygen. This was a very common practice to expand their capacity in using less energy.

Another great breathing technique to expand your energy capacity is the "four breaths in" concept. You exhale completely and then breathe in with four equally strong breaths—through your nose—to fill your lungs. Then let your air out in one long deep continuous exhale and repeat. This is a great energizing technique, which can stimulate your brain cells and heighten awareness.

These are just a few breathing techniques. Like anything else, they should be practiced everyday. You should be consistent and attempt to continuously expand your capacity. Start with three minutes. Slowly build to 10, 20 and 30 minutes. These breathing techniques can be used to enhance any art, activity, sport, or performance.

The basic concept to enhancing any sport, art, movement or activity is breathing with movement. If you are painting, extend your breathing and an image of energy through your arms and fingers, right through the brush and onto the canvas. After you breathe in, visualize and generate your breath in an energy state to the spot about three inches below your navel point. Imagine this center as a small sun or ball of energy, building up intensity. Then focus your breath in a visualized energy state through whatever movement you are doing. If you are playing basketball, focus your energy through your arms. It should come out your fingers; go right through the ball and all the way to the basket or whatever your target is. Imagine that energy is a laser beam; this will increase your accuracy.

If you are fighting, practicing karate or some martial art, focus your breathing from that point. Channel it through your hips, and into your strike, attack or technique. Focus that energy right through your knuckles ... a laser beam right through the target you are aiming at and through your opponent. If you are executing a basic block, such as a down block, imagine that energy, through your breathing, extending through your arms and fingers, extending 50 feet through the room, as if extending your block to 50 feet and cutting the room in half. If you are shooting a weapon, extend that breath energy from your hands and palms, right through the barrel of the gun to your target, like a laser beam. If you practice this type of breathing and integrate it into everything you do, you can immensely increase your accuracy and performance.

If you have one major secret and ability you are totally in control of in this life, it's your breath. And breath can change the state of your mind and body almost instantly. You can use your breath to make your body as hard as steel. You can also use it to make your body soft and supple like a willow. Your breath can make your body heavy, like a very large liberty bell. It can also make your body light, like a piece of cotton. Your breathing will change your mental state and that will change the state of your body.

It is common knowledge that drivers under the influence of alcohol often don't get hurt badly when they get into major accidents because they are so relaxed. You can also make your mind and body incredibly sensitive and aware through your breathing. Imagine you are extending your breathing out, all around your body like the energy from an aura, uniting it with nature and everything around you. Imagine sensing and feeling everything that comes into your field. Then do the opposite. Contract your feeling. Make your breathing small and shallow, like you barely exist. Attempt to shrink your breathing down to nothing and imagine you are not there ... you are invisible. Yogis slow their heartbeats down in a similar manner.

If you want to calm your mind, first calm your breathing and don't think. People subconsciously use breathing to help them walk on fire, swords, glass and execute other feats. It is obvious how proper control of your breathing can enhance everything you want to accomplish. The proper recipe is breathing, the right mental state, feeling and imagery.

In the Special Training chapter, recall the endurance the Tendai Buddhist marathon monks of Mount Hiei acquire through their training and conditioning. One of their secrets to accomplishing these superhuman feats, besides their mentality, is proper and specialized breathing techniques. As mentioned, they get hardly any sleep. They have to learn how to relax certain parts of their bodies, so they can rejuvenate them while they are on the move and jogging. They focus their breathing through those parts of the body, attempting to rejuvenate them in the most useful order. They use their breathing to get their bodies, mind and energy to work in the most economical way. They attempt to relax, take excess power and tension out of various sections of the body while moving. They learn to sleep a few moments while sitting or standing. Sometimes these monks will grab a few winks of sleep or rest while jogging lightly, meditating or waiting for a traffic light.

The monks will also harmonize their movement with the rhythm of a chant or mantra while they are jogging. The chanting creates an efficient rhythm in their breathing so they can acquire the most energy for the best economy of movement. The monks coordinate the rhythm and depth of their breathing with the terrain. They take deep breaths from their lower abdomens when they climb, step high or ascend. Many of these monks use another ancient breathing rhythm technique to cover long distances efficiently. They would inhale with two short breaths through their nose and exhale with one longer one through the nose. This is an economical way to jog and breathe. They also coordinate the rhythm of their breaths with imagery and visualization. They might imagine their bodies to be as light as a feather and they would lightly flow through the woods and mountains. The monks' incredible mental focus and concentration also help them keep a rhythm with their breathing. They practice staring and focusing on a distant star not allowing their minds to wander or become distracted. They don't let any thoughts come up; sometimes they do not even blink for long periods of time. Through the years, there have been many Tibetan and Mongolia recordings of sightings of these monks bounding through the woods and mountains. They were said to be able to keep moving for 48 hours and cover more than 200 miles.

Years ago, I used to raise American pit bull terriers, which are commonly known as fighting dogs. They are born with an extraordinary natural fighting spirit. My male dog's name was Algonquin, after the Algonquin Indians. On one occasion, he got out and was running after a wild stray dog. I saw a van coming, and he didn't, because he was running between the cars across the street. I could see what was going to happen and couldn't do anything about it. He ran right out in front of the van, and the driver didn't even have time to put the brakes on. The van was going about 35 mph. The van's front bumper hit him in the head and ran directly over him. I saw his body flipping under the van. Then I saw the back rear tire run over him. I thought for a moment that Algonquin was going to be smashed on the pavement. When the dog flipped out from the back of the van, he landed on his feet and continued to run after the other dog. He was running slower though. I caught up to him and started to check his external injuries. He was limping and had a chunk of meat out of his brow. I turned him on his side and saw a tire track across part of his chest and stomach. I thought, "Oh my God! His ribs must be broken and he has to have all kinds of internal damage!" Most pit bulls don't show pain, so I thought this has got to be much worse than it looks and he's not showing it. I couldn't believe he was still alive after all that. I took him to the veterinarian hospital, and he had to stay there for three days, so they could analyze all of the damage and injuries. I was expecting all kinds of internal damage and that he would not live long. It took the doctor three days to check everything out at the hospital. The final diagnosis was a fractured bone in his paw and laceration in his brow, but he did not have any serious internal damage. I couldn't believe it, because I saw what happened. For months, I tried to figure how and why he could have survived. Of course, it could have been a miracle, if everything was aligned and timed perfectly, so the impact missed the vital organs. Algonquin's body was like steel, because I ran him 10 to 12 miles a day for many years. Then it hit me. Maybe his natural fighting instinct executed the best type of exhale to help repel the impact.

Chapter 16
Powerful Ki, Chi Generating Principles

The Japanese word for life force is ki, in Chinese, chi. In Sanskrit, it is prana. Aiki, in Japanese, means "united harmony of life force." In Japanese, do means way. When you put them together, as in the martial art (aikido), it means, "The united way of harmony life force energy." This is using the flow of your energy field and your opponent's to your advantage to defeat him.

Kiai, as mentioned earlier, means spirit shout or concentrated focus of life force energy. The Japanese word for illness has two characters or symbols. One means illness and the other means, ki. The Japanese and the Chinese both associate the ki with health. This subtle energy is in and around us all the time. It can reflect a positive or negative atmosphere internally or externally.

Internal energy, in your body and mind, is continuously circulating through your major organs, limbs, mentality and consciousness. This energy is also connected to your nervous system and pressure points. It is in you all the time. Sometimes it cycles faster other times slower, depending on your mentality and overall health. You can increase the amount of internal energy you

Tsutomu Ohshima generating a powerful energy around him.
He is waiting until the last split-second before he moves.

have or you can decrease it. These internal and external cycles of energy or ki are all tied into your basic aura.

There is also ki or chi all around us. Nature has its own energy, subtle and similar to yours. Nature, plants, animals, water and rocks also have their own energy, and a combination of these energies creates other specific atmospheres. These too can represent a more positive (plus or negative) minus atmosphere, which human beings have the awareness to sense and pick up on. We can even use these energies from various types of alignments, colors, objects and shapes of objects to create a specific type of atmosphere in our homes, yards, gardens or businesses.

There is a Chinese art thousands of years old, which specializes in this; called Feng Shui. This chi energy has been an established, accepted fact to the Chinese for thousands of years. The healing system of acupuncture is also largely based on it through the manipulation of pressure points with special acupuncture needles. Acupuncture has grown to be a widely accepted healing method today in many countries and cultures and has had a wide degree of success. Chinese believe that when people get sick or injured the chi energy gets blocked in certain areas, inhibiting the healing and the flow of energy. Stimulating these pressure points with acupuncture needles breaks down the blockage and the chi energy can begin to flow more normally.

Your breathing and your ki are closely connected. You can use your breathing to alter your ki or energy through the various breathing exercises and concepts mentioned in the breathing chapter. Your ki will be focused anywhere you concentrate your breathing. You imagine that energy, as you did with your breathing, traveling through your body wherever you want to your benefit.

Let's look at the ki-generating breath previously introduced in a little more detail. You fill up your lungs, from lower to upper, then slowly exhale out your nose with you mouth closed. Your tongue is on your upper palate. You compress and hold the air or exhale back in the rear of your throat. It will make a sound similar to a teapot building up steam. You can make this sound very subtle or extremely intense, depending on how strong you would like to make the energy. Everyone has a different capacity, depending on his mentality and health.

As noted, the ki can be concentrated in the lower portion of your abdomen, about three inches below your navel point. The Japanese, call this the tanden energy center. A good technique is to first generate ki in this point as you inhale. Then you can channel this energy any place you would like, internally or externally, from that tanden energy point.

There is a certain recipe for to generating more ki. You first need an open mind. You must at least be open to the possibility that this ki energy exists and you can direct it. It doesn't mean that ki doesn't exist if you don't believe it. But a minus attitude will not encourage you to search. When you do believe that ki exists, you create a strong plus atmosphere and you will automatically be able to develop and generate more ki.

You must have the right mentality to generate more ki. It is more beneficial to have a general positive attitude about life and yourself. You should have strong self-confidence but not be egotistical. If you are negative and have many mental blocks and psychological issues, that will create a minus to the vibration and atmosphere of the ki. The proper type of mentality and attitude, along with the correct type of breathing, will help to generate more ki.

When you breathe the appropriate way, it will relax your body, so the ki can flow better and more freely. To develop ki, it is better to have a relaxed, subconsciously controlled body. Of course tapping into subconscious energy (by first letting go of conscious power) takes practice and is a many-year work in progress.

There is a special way to tense your muscles and generate ki, but you still have to create the appropriate mentality. The Shaolin monks use this type of strong, intense breathing with a tense limb or body part to break boards over their limbs. Nevertheless, it is better to get your ki to flow by being relaxed but extremely focused. Then focus your mind and your breathing where you want the ki to go or how you want to use it.

Thoughts affect your ki flow instantly. When you have strong, positive thoughts, your ki will automatically be positive and strong. These thoughts will automatically affect the strength of your physical body, including movement and technique. Negative thoughts, create a negative or minus vibration in your ki or energy field. This too will dramatically affect the state of your physical body, movement and technique. You will become much weaker, despite doing everything outwardly the same, because of that negative thought you had while you executed the movement. It has been said that nine-tenths of all diseases are psychosomatic in origin.

That negative thought and the subsequent result may not be

too important and noticeable at a novice level, but they can be crucial at a professional or expert level. It could mean life or death in a combat, situation. In Western culture, it is always said that positive thinking is better than negative thinking. Zen teachers say that no thinking is better than even positive thinking. Since the mushin or no-mind mentality opens you to the universe. When you don't think, your mentality is more neutral and unbiased. When you don't think and are unbiased, your mind doesn't have any limitations or mental blocks and your execution is not filtered through any biased thoughts. This is different from the technique of visualizing your technique or movement perfectly.

Tsutomu Ohshima exhibiting a very calm strong state of mind, while being attacked with a kick.

Visualization comes way before this final performance. You visualize an execution so many times that your subconscious mind eventually files that movement at a deep level in your mind. When you actually execute the technique, you are performing it from your subconscious mind and not thinking about it. If you want to get the most out of your execution, it is better to acquire the no-mind or no-thought mentality. That mentality will tap you right into your previously visualized programmed subconscious mind.

You can hold so much information and data in your mind and memory, but you can only think one basic thought at a time.

Tsutomu Ohshima and senior Toshio Kamata-Watanabe,
present at a celebration karate exchange practice,
at Cal Tech University in Pasadena.

It may seem like a lot more, but in that specific moment, it is one thought, even if it is just for a split second. That thought can be an actual thought on some specific thing or it can be a no-mind, no-thought focus on nothing. It is sometimes referred to the gap, which is the space in between your thoughts. When you first train your subconscious mind repetitively and then acquire the no-mind mentality, you are in one of the best mental states to stimulate your ki to flow.

Chinese culture also emphasizes that ki or internal energy is extremely important for an individual's health. Chinese believe that if an individual's ki becomes too minus that person will eventually get sick or have an accident. Another person with a much stronger ki can heal a person who doesn't have enough ki. The person who is healthy channels and focuses his strong ki to wherever the person with the weaker ki needs it. This needs to be done until the sick person's ki can eventually flow stronger and take over. It may take a number of treatments, depending on how diminished, the sick person's ki is. The healing also depends on the strength and focus of the healthy person's ki. If the ki keeps on becoming more minus, eventually death will occur. It is very hard to help someone who has not taken care of him or herself for a long time and has acquired a serious illness or disease. Even a healthy person with strong ki will not be able to help. The sick person has undergone too much damage over a long period of time and that usually cannot be reversed. But there have been exceptions. Sometimes, even when an individual is in a serious stage of illness, changing his attitude to a much more positive one can really help. The positive attitude will change the flow and effect of his ki, so it is much more beneficial. It is now easier to understand why the Japanese use the two characters to describe illness, as mentioned earlier.

The Japanese word kokoro was discussed earlier. When an individual acquires this kind of mentality, he can generate tremendous spirit. He has no fear of dying; at the same time, he will not surrender or ever give up. You can see how this kind of mentality can generate incredible ki. When an individual's mentally is not attached to dying, he can ultimately express himself and not have any mental blocks to hold himself back. There have been numerous stories of great warriors throughout history who exhibited this same type of mentality. They have faced innumerable odds and survived. Many others who expressed this type of mentality in battle didn't survive but ended up making an incredible difference in turning the battle the other way or saving many people. In Eastern culture, they would say, in either case, it was heaven's will.

Chapter 17

The Creativity of Perceptions Using them to Evolve Consciousness

Perception is probably the most common and varied mental element utilized. Perception has and covers a huge capacity. It can cover a vast spectrum of information. Perceptions, is therefore also the source of illusion. Your perception is created from a broad range of influences, which may include, race, nationality, tradition, education, genetic elements and experiences, etc. The list of contributing elements is endless. All of these topics can influence various types of perceptions. Any of these factors and combinations of them, to different degrees, can be more dominant in their influence than others.

Two people from different countries—raised in completely separate cultures, religions and political traditions – are apt to have quite different perceptions of life. It is also interesting to note that two people who live in the same country, state and city—and might even live right next door to each other—may also have completely different perceptions of life. And the opposite might be true. Two people from different countries, cultures and traditions might have very similar perceptions in many things.

Perception has helped to create and discover some of the most important advances to mankind. It has also created some of the most terrible wars, battles, disasters and harm to the human race. Intelligence, mentality, attitude, intuition, creativeness and consciousness can fuel perception. Hatred, fear, selfishness, greediness and egomania—or specific combinations of any of these—can also ignite it. One of the most limited ways to create a perception of a topic would be with a very fundamental, limited amount of information, data and knowledge. The hardest way to evolve your consciousness would be to create a specific perception with incorrect or wrong information, data and knowledge.

This adds to the reasons why perception is one of the most interesting abilities you have. Perception can be used for the highest good or for the most selfish gratification. In fact, many of you will perceive what I am saying right now in numerous ways. Some will agree and many will disagree, based on where your perception is coming from and what it is based on. A simple example would be when five people witness a car accident, robbery or a fight. Let's say that all of them are standing in different positions, viewing the incident from different angles and timings. Each of the five people would have a little different view of exactly what they saw. They wouldn't necessarily be right or wrong, but they all viewed it from a different angle or have a varied interpretation of the same event. The most interesting element about it is that they all viewed the incident from different conditioned mentalities and varied pre-conditioned mental patterns. This perception is filtered through an individual's mentality. The perception of an event, incident, situation or experience has to be filtered through that person's education, race, nationality, religion, political faction, intelligence, experiences, bias, likes and dislikes. Sometimes it is one of these; other times it is a combination. This perception, which has been filtered through this mentality to make a decision or judgment, can be varied to numerous perspectives and degrees.

In most cases, and especially dealing with the masses of people, there are certain basic concepts that are adhered to in mak-

Gichen Funakoshi (1868 to 1957).
Master Funakoshi was the first individual to introduce
empty-hand karate to Japan in 1916.

Tom Muzila discussing a topic with Tsutomu Ohshima.
Ohshima-Sensei trained directly under
Master Funakoshi for latter part of his life.

ing most decisions, judgments, criticisms and analyses. These elements will be generally filtered through an individual's mentality, which consists of all their learned information, data, knowledge and experiences in life. It is extremely difficult for a person not to be very biased or prejudiced when he analyzes information and experiences. He makes a decision that a situation is right, wrong, good, bad, hard, easy, etc. You can see this in many aspects and experiences of life. The main one would be with a man and a woman who become husband and wife. The husband perceives something a specific way and the wife perceives the information, data and situation in a completely different way. Usually, either one is not totally right or wrong; they both perceive that information from completely different mentalities.

Perception is evident in all aspects of life, including religions, politics, race, nationalities and cultures. Most people cannot understand why another person has different views; in most cases, causes friction, disagreement, arguments and fighting. It is very evident simply raising children. When they become teenagers, many of them think they know more than their parents. They just can't understand why their parents won't agree with them. The children have not experienced what the parents have, so they have a completely different perception of reality.

Today, it is also so obvious how biased the news and media are, too. It is very hard for them to report basic facts without putting their own slant on it. A good example of radically different perceptions would be with an individual who was raised in a free democratic society and a terrorist. It is amazing how perception from past experiences and knowledge can justify almost anything, such as killing innocent women, children and even their own people. These people can commit selfish acts, go back to their own families like nothing happened, and are actually praised for it by their own communities. The majority of people have their own reasons to justify their own causes, regardless of how radical they are.

There have been many psychological tests done to prove that even looks make a difference in opinions. If a man or women is better looking, more handsome or prettier than others, most people will tend to favor the better-looking person. It is especially pertinent in political elections. This is more evident if people are undecided about their choice. Most people are only attracted to three aspects of the candidates in an election, and those are the visual, auditory and kinesthetic capabilities. If a person is subconsciously biased towards visuals or looks, he will lean more towards the candidate who looks better. Another person might be subconsciously attracted to the way a candidate talks, so that will sway his vote towards that person. The last category would be an individual who is subconsciously impressed with the way a candidate uses his body and hands when he gives a speech. That person will more likely vote for the candidate who is more kinesthetic.

All of this usually first happens at a subconscious level. Then their subconscious mind alters their conscious mind to analyze and justify the reasons and logic for having these opinions. Many people become and are fundamental type thinkers. There are many things that are black and white, but most things are not. You can imagine what can happen if a very biased fundamental thinker acquires an immense amount of power and authority. This person will attempt to project his mentality, views and opinions on everyone else and try to influence them. This happens all of the time. Jim Jones influenced all of his followers in Guyana to commit suicide. Of course, the worse one was Hitler. It is very easy to influence people when their minds have been programmed, trained and conditioned this way their entire life. People influenced so easily are usually ones who are insecure and looking for something to identify with in life. They are very predictable, influenced easily and follow the masses.

There is another level or spectrum of perception. It is the difference in having a higher or lower mentality or consciousness. This is a simple way to state it. It is basically the difference in a more mature, responsible, open-minded and unattached individual and one who isn't. The person with a higher mentality sees the bigger, more long-range picture. This person makes much better choices for himself and everyone around him. It is also a person who benefits the whole, rather than just himself. This individual could be a specialist in any job, business, profession or art. Many times these types of individuals end up being very positive role models and leaders in society.

An individual with a lower mentality would be more self-oriented and only see the short-term benefits. He would not be able to consider how his actions or choices would affect him and everyone around him in the long range. He would also let and get negative emotions involved with his judgments. He would be adding more fuel to the fire when he let passionate, negative emotions get involved with his decisions.

The majority of people make their judgments according to how they feel. Emotions and feelings are relative and illusions are made up. When people always use emotions to make the majority of decisions, it is very hard to change. It all depends on what type of emotions they are. If they are making decisions and solving problems from a very joyful well-being state of mind, their choices will be much better and at a higher level for everyone. If they make choices from very negative, selfish, greedy resentful emotions, they will eventually hurt themselves and everyone around them.

The real bias and prejudice with people is not related to race, nationality, religion, politics or cultures. The real prejudice is between people's mentality and consciousness. A person with a higher mentality has the ability to first see things from other people's points of view. He also has a more open mentality to see and understand his own point of view, but he will not be mentally attached to it. He attempts to see and feel how it is, to be in the other person's shoes or situation. When he gets a sense of that, he can acquire a better understanding of where the other individual is coming from in his views. This is the first step in acquiring a better understanding with that person or situation.

You are in a much better state to negotiate and acquire harmony with another person or situation when you have that rapport. This friction happens continuously on many different levels. It happens with countries, religions, political issues, business negotiations, parents, children, and husbands and wives. It is the same on every level. The same mistakes people make in their perceptions with countries are the same mistakes husbands and wives makes when talking to each other.

When it comes down to it, everything you make up or create in your mind is really an illusion. You create these beliefs, philosophies, concepts, principles, judgments, identities and opinions based on what you have learned and experienced in life. You also base them on what other people and individuals have told you. You create all of these views, which you end up basing your whole lives on and everything you do. But, is it true? It is more of a relative truth, based on your particular situation. It may not be true for anyone else, though.

The majority of people live their whole lives relating to this illusion they have created in their mind. This illusion can make us very successful or it can put many restrictions on us, too. It usually causes tremendous friction in our lives and holds us back from getting what we truly want. It really comes down this. We can make anything real that you want. We create our whole identity of whom we are based on these illusions we make up in our mind. This illusion or identity may or may not manifest physically, but we create those beliefs, philosophies, concepts, understandings, mental blocks, insecurities, judgments, criticisms and fears in our mind. We give and feed them energy and reality. Is this, who you really are at a very deep level? Are you just a doctor, lawyer, law enforcement officer or president of a corporation? This is also related and why it is so hard for people to forgive. They can't let go of the anger or resentment they have for an individual. The only person who is truly hurting when you hold onto this anger and energy and stay attached to it is yourself. You feed and keep that energy and vibration bottled up inside your mind, which eventually spreads out to your body. It is all connected through your nervous system. Many times that negative vibration of resentfulness in your mind will eventually create a disease or major problem in your life.

How can you mentally rise above this illusion? It sounds very simple, but it is incredibly hard to do, because people do not want to let go of their attachments, egos and identities. When you are young, you can become very opinionated, because of your beliefs. Hopefully, as you get older and more mature, you tend to be able to see other points of view. You have to be much more open-minded and not be so quick to judge and criticize.

There is usually some information or facet of the situation or problem you don't know or see.

If you study the lives of so-called true enlightened masters, you will see that they all have many common traits. However, you first have to understand what a true enlightened master is before you can study his common traits. This is relative and a matter of perception, too. You would have to agree on certain traits to help categorize them. It is an individual who first attempts to master him or herself. He attempts to challenge and face himself against all of his weakness, fears, mental blocks, issues and insecurities. This is a person who sacrifices himself for the benefit of others. He doesn't take advantage of other people's weaknesses. He is a unique individual, very humble and independent, but strong. You could write a whole chapter or even book of some ideals of a true master, but these are some basic common traits, which is a foundation from which to work.

Let's talk about some more specific abilities, characteristics and mental traits. A true master is a master of himself and also his consciousness. He is free and liberated mentally. His mind is not attached to materialistic elements. He has no limits in his mind of what he can do and what can be accomplished, but he is very realistic, rational and down-to-earth, too. He doesn't force anything on people, including data, information, concepts or philosophies. He would only communicate if a student genuinely wanted to know or learn something and were ready for it. The master wouldn't force anything on anyone, unless he felt it was the best time to commit and put his foot down for justice. This would only be if it were a benefit to all.

How does all of this relate to a warrior's or peak performance mentality? It comes back to the concept that has been emphasized throughout the whole book. The fewer mental blocks, fears, insecurities, bias, judgments and attachments you have, the more you will be able to express yourself clearly and uninhibitedly in battle, competition, performances, sports, arts and professions. In other words, you will be able to express yourself to unlimited boundaries and levels in whatever you are practicing, training and expressing. There will be no friction in your subconscious and conscious mind to hold you back. You will be totally free, liberated and have an unlimited mentally.

I remember hearing a story many years ago when I was practicing a lot of kundalini yoga. It was about a Sikh warrior who had survived a battle in India a few hundred years ago. There were numerous soldiers dead, injured and wounded on the battlefield—from both armies. The Sikh warrior started aiding and helping many of his wounded soldiers. After a period of time, when he had enough help aiding his soldiers, he started aiding and helping the wounded and injured soldiers from the enemy army. One of his commanding officers yelled at him, "What are you doing? You are aiding and helping the enemy wounded soldiers?" The Sikh warrior yelled back, "What are you talking about? He is still a spirited warrior and deserves to be helped." The Silk warrior obviously had no mental blocks, judgments, bias and attachments. His profession and commitment was to fight the enemy army, but he did not hate or resent them. It was his job and he performed it to the best of his ability. When the battle was over, his empathic nature took over to not only help his own soldiers, but to just help human beings, which happened to be the enemy soldiers.

There is a famous story in the Chinese Chan Buddhist tradition. Hui-Neng was the 28th patriarch or master in transition from the Buddha in India. Originally, he was a janitor in the monastery that he meditated in. One day the master of that monastery had a practice in which the monks or students would all have to write an answer to a question, something such as, "What is enlightenment?" The most popular monk of the monastery had a very beautiful creative answer, which all the other monks were impressed with. Hui-Neng was in the back of the main meditation room and heard his answer. He respectfully disagreed with it. Basically, he was saying how all of these things could be true when everything is really an illusion. The other monks didn't understand Hui-Neng's answer, but the master recognized his understanding. Shortly after, the master died. Hui-Neng left the monastery and the popular monk became the master. No one heard from Hui-Neng for about 15 years.

Some 15 years later, at another monastery in China, three monks were walking back to that monastery on a trail. The monastery came in view and there was a flag flapping in the wind on the top of it. The monk on the right said, "Look, the flag is moving." The monk on the left said, "No! The wind is moving." The monk in the middle said, very calmly, "Your mind is moving!" They discovered later that was Hui-Neng.

Chapter 18

Develop Effective Practical Intuition

Intuition is an innate human trait. We all have a certain amount of abilities. Numerous people believe in it and many others do not. It does boost your intuitive powers if you do believe in them, like anything else. If you don't believe in yourself or any ability you have, you won't be as effective. If you don't believe in intuition or psychic abilities, it doesn't mean you don't have these. You still have it and it is activated to a certain degree. You might be attributing a certain decision to knowledge or reason, but you may have decided on something, because of an intuition you had.

There are numerous psychic abilities, such as telepathy, psychometry, precognition, retro-cognition, spirit photography, automatic writing, clairvoyance, clairaudienancy, scrying, crystal gazing, psychic healing, dowsing, aura reading, psychokinesis, remote viewing, astral projection and even levitation and teleportation. The list can go on. There are so many categories, but they are all connected to each other in some way. Intuition, psychic attributes and electromagnetic sensitivity is natural for all animals, fish, birds and insects, to some degree. People are sensitive and intuitive to many things in different ways. People also perceive and interpret their intuition abilities all in a personal way.

This is a vast field and topic. It is also hard to separate the authentic people from the limited ability ones and the phonies. It is harder to separate the people who are right and wrong 50 percent of the time. Sometimes they are making it up and other times they are right on and happen to be accurate. We all have the abilities to be correct and right at least 50 percent of the time. If we all practiced these abilities, like we practice sports or numerous other arts and skills, we would have a tremendous capacity. Like sports or other attributes, some people are very naturally sensitive and don't have to practice much at all. It is genetic. Others have to practice extremely hard before they acquire a certain degree of sensitivity, which is effective. This field is like any other field. It is all a matter of level. In any field, there are only two, three or maybe five percent of the people who are incredibly accurate. We would call these people extremely high-level individuals in those skills. Again, this goes for every field, including doctors, lawyers, dancers, yogis, martial artists, or soldiers, etc. Would you rather work with someone who is 75 or 97 percent accurate?

In various fields, arts and professions, individuals naturally use a certain degree of their sensitivity or psychic abilities to aid in their profession. Some realize that they are using it and many others don't realize they are using it to help aid some aspect of their profession. When people like or love each other very much, they end up being much more sensitive to each other's needs, and the emotional and mental states. They naturally project their feelings or sensitivity to encompass the other person's aura or consciousness. They become more integrated mentally with their partner's or mate's mind, which enables them to have a better sense of what the mate is feeling. It comes down to sensing energies or fluctuations in energy levels and what type of emotion or mental state is categorizing that energy. This could be positive or negative emotions and energies. The strongest element to pick up on is how strong and intense the energy and emotion is that an individual is expressing. If a person is exhibiting a very strong emo-

*Don Depree expressing a strong focused
and confident mentality, before engaging
his opponent at the Melrose dojo.*

tion and energy, it is going to be easier to pick up on. Of course, it also depends on the sensitivity of the person receiving the energy. If you have an individual who is attempting to receive the energy but is not sensitive at all or very numb to it, he will not be able to feel or pick up on anything at all. If you have a person who is not putting out very much emotion and energy, a person who is extremely sensitive and psychic will still be able to pick up on it. You basically need a connection of energy, no matter who is more sensitive. It can almost be compared to sending and receiving radio signals. It really breaks down to receivers and senders. Some people are great senders, but they are not very good receivers and vise versa. Some people are also great at both. Then it depends on the degree of how sensitive they are. For example, if you have a sender who can put out 75 percent energy but a receiver who can only sense 15 percent energy, there is still a gap of 10 percent. If you have a weak sender who can only put out about 20 percent energy but an extremely strong receiver who can pick up 90 percent, then you are possibly going to have a good connection between them. This also goes vise versa, too. These percentages can fluctuate with the same individuals at different times. This also can depend on the mental state and mood of the individual. Another opposite example of this would be an individual putting out no or hardly any thoughts or energy from his minds. This could be a person who is in a very calm meditative mental state. If we take this a step further, it would be like a ninja in old Japan, trying to hide in a castle and be totally undetected on every level. He would attempt to have no thoughts in his mind, so it wouldn't put out an energy signal that any presence was there. If a ninja were in a very active beta mental state with much emotional energy behind it, it would be mentally easier for another sensitive samurai or warrior to pick up on his presence.

There is also another important factor. No matter how sensitive and strong a sender and receiver is, he has to be able to somehow get taped into that exact person's energy field or vibration. Everything has a certain vibration, which vibrates at a specific frequency. And the list includes everything from a rock, bowl of water, piece of wood, rock, color, bird, fish, animal, and especially each and every human being. Somehow you must get tuned into that person's specific vibration to tap right into his personal field, aura, emotions and energy field. Each part of our brain, mind, thoughts, organs and every system of our bodies all has a specific vibration, depending on condition. All of those vibrations integrated together create an overall electromagnetic vibration, which is sometimes referred to as our aura. We need something that vibrates at that same level or is able to channel that vibration to us to better be able to pick up on that specific vibration. We are bombarded each day and every moment with so many different kinds of vibrations, data and information, and it is quite hard to separate them from each other. If we have all these, vibrations and energy fields projected at us each day— from person, places, situations and thoughts—how are we going to know what we are picking up on? This is where another big confusion comes into play in the psychic realms. Are these our thoughts or are they the thoughts of another person? It is hard enough to decipher whether we are making up something logically in our minds or picking it up from another person. So, you can see why someone has to have an incredible amount of practice and experience to be able to decipher the differences they are getting from all the different types of energy, data and information we are constantly receiving.

This is something referred to as "a witness is involved." In psychometry, this is the ability to pick up or read personal objects of a specific person, object, area or situation. Psychometry is probably the most naturally used and popular existing psychic ability. More people utilize this psychic ability naturally, without realizing it, more than any other psychic ability. Most people continually express getting certain types of feelings from this person, place, area or situation all the time. If a person has worn a personal object, say a watch, ring, necklace or bracelet for a long time, that object absorbs the personal vibration of that person.

Senior Isao Obata studying his bokken.

There are many elements, which could be used as a witness or in place of a personal object, such as another person, a photo or signature. When you have something personal from that person to actually tune into, your sensitivity has a vibration it can directly resonate with.

The eyes of another person are one of the best things for a warrior, fighter or martial artist to tap into so he can learn or sense anything about his opponent. As mentioned earlier, the eyes are a reflection of a person's soul, spirit, subconscious mind and thoughts. By gazing deep into one's eyes, you also gaze into his mind and have the ability to sense how he feels and thinks. You can also sense when he is going to attack. The eyes can transmit a large degree of energy and presence. Many people have been in a situation in which they thought they were alone somewhere, but they had the strangest feeling that someone was looking at them or watching them. They were picking up on the transmission of presence and energy from another person's eyes. Many sensitive hunters have also had this experience when they knew an animal was watching them, but they couldn't see the animal. Later, when the animal finally showed itself, they found out they were right.

People will naturally be more sensitive to pick up on very subtle energies and signals if they are in a calm alpha mental state. The right brain, as mentioned earlier, is the creative and emotional hemisphere. When you are in that relaxed calm mental state and expand your awareness, it will aid your right brain to better switch on and be utilized. It is easy to practice these psychic abilities in your daily lives. Expand your awareness, attempt to put yourself inside of other people's minds and practice to feel what they are feeling and thinking. If you get direct energy contact with them, it should easily come up in your mind. It is extremely important to first learn how to empty and clear your own mind. Then it will usually be the first thoughts or feelings that come up in your mind. Every time you start to walk around a corner, open a door or get to some kind of hallway intersection, try to sense if there is another person's presence there. Every time the phone rings try to sense the person who is calling. Before a person speaks, try to anticipate what he is going to say. When you go into a building, nightclub, restaurant, neighborhood or any kind of an area, put your antennas out there and sense what type of energies and atmosphere you are picking up on. Is it calm, peaceful, stressful, threatening or dangerous? Always remember and take a mental note of the feeling you had just before you gave an answer. What was the feeling you had when you were right and even the feeling you have when you were wrong or off? Start remembering and aligning yourself with the feeling you had every time you were correct on something. Eventually, your awareness and sensitivity will continually respond from your subconscious mind and not your conscious mind. You will not have to think about it that often.

If you are an individual who has a more threatening and dangerous profession or job, such as a law enforcement officer, firefighter or soldier in combat, your intuitive abilities will become extremely heightened if you use them and concentrate on them. If you are a police officer and an individual really hates you, this is a strong energy being projected at you which is available to pick up on. When your life is on the line, your sensitivity and psychic abilities will be generated to an incredible degree. It is also your built-in alarm system.

There is new evidence from a scientific study, which supports that our brain has a built in early warning system to detect danger. There is a region in the brain, known as the anterior cingulated cortex or (ACC), which is located in the front of the brain. Activity greatly increases there, especially when people have to solve difficult problems or make decisions. After analysis, it was determined that this portion of the brain can decipher when we are about to make a decision, which is a mistake. Joshua Brown, Ph.D. and a research associate in psychology at Washington University in St. Louis, states in a news release. "The ACC appears to act as an early warning system; it learns to warn us in advance when our behavior might lead to a negative outcome, so that we are able to be more careful and avoid making a mistake."

Another recent study showed that the brain can also quickly detect the various meanings of expressions on our faces. There is a natural reaction to our minds, eyes and face when we feel fear or are scared. It was found that the human brain can instantly recognize fear in another persons eyes. Paul J. Whalen, MD, lead researcher and a professor of psychiatry and psychology at the University of Wisconsin at Madison, said that it happens before anything is said. That scared eye and look automatically triggers an ancient response in the brain. This phenomenon occurs in a portion of the brain called the amygdala. This is the region where emotions are processed, such as fear, stress, anxiety, joy and lust.

If you truly want to become more sensitive and aware, there are endless drills and practices to do. Try doing a majority of things in the dark. They don't have to be complicated things, but just simple ones. Try walking around in total darkness in your house. Try getting dressed in total darkness. Eventually, practice karate or execute a portion of the sport activity you do in the dark. If you're a karate practitioner or a fighter, practice kata or forms in the dark or hit a heavy bag with a blindfold on. Execute some light sparring or engagement drills in the dark or with a blindfold on. Just by imaging that you are a blind person and attempting to do many basic activities throughout the day safely will considerably expand your awareness and sensitivity abilities.

When I was in the Special Forces, I spent a lot of time out in the jungles, especially at night. I eventually became pretty comfortable at night, especially knowing that the enemy couldn't see me. For years, I used to climb a lot of mountains and also spent a lot of time out in the woods and forests at night. That also became pretty comfortable. I read something, years ago, on how important it is for a warrior to sensitize his peripheral vision. This information mentioned that we had the ability to actually see a bit beyond the natural vision of light spectrum through sensitizing our peripheral vision. I thought I would try practicing it for a while and see what happened. I got some ski-type sunglasses and put white paper in the lens of both eyes, so I couldn't see straight ahead. I would attempt to do certain activities and make it through the day, without tripping, falling or walking into something. I did this for quite a few months and really noticed a huge spectrum of awareness being sharpened. I felt as if I didn't really have to see anything right ahead of me and my peripheral vision became incredibly enhanced. I became very comfortable with it in most activities. I felt it also helped to give me a very complete awareness of not only what was happening to the sides of me, but also to the rear and the front. Eventually, I was able to climb a smaller mountain with those sunglasses on; I just relied on my peripheral vision. I don't recommend that any of you do this, unless you are supervised.

Year ago I attended a yoga intensive Special Training. It was up in the mountains at about 7,200 feet. We only slept about three hours a night and woke up extremely early. We performed yoga for about 12 hours a day and ate only fruits and vegetarian food. The yoga Special Training was 10 days long, and we could only speak audibly with our actual voice on the first day. We couldn't talk for the remaining nine days. We had to use other means to communicate. We were executing intensive breathing and chanting exercises continuously in three-hour sessions. I felt a very noticeable sensitivity increase by the fourth day. By the ninth and tenth day, I felt incredibly sensitive and at many times felt a presence of someone behind me. I would turn around, see someone there, and notice he was still at least 50 feet behind me. I felt like my sensitivity, awareness or aura had expanded to more than 50 feet from this type of training.

There was a top samurai family in the 1600s called the Yagyu family. Yagyu Jubei was considered one of the top sword masters around. Yagyu was the brother of the Shogun's fencing sword teacher. He was probably the strongest swordsman in his family. He was also considered to be extreme in his training and personal philosophy. Many people misinterpreted him as being cruel and blood-thirsty. Yagyu Jubei just wanted to be the best swordsmen around and not have any mental blocks or attachments. He lived at the same time as Miyamoto Musashi. Musashi and Jubei had never met, but they were well aware of each other. In those days, there were no photos or paintings of these swordsmen, so they did not know what the other looked like. There was a story that became popular later about when these two met briefly. It took place near the Nagoya Castle. One swordsman was walking down a street one way, while the other was approaching from the opposite way. As they approached, they both stopped about 30 feet from each other. One man said, "You are Yagu Jubei." Yagyu replied, "You are Miyamoto Musashi." They continued and walked slowly past each other. It is interesting that neither had seen the other before, but they both immediately recognized each other from their presence.

It is extremely important for a warrior, fighter or top professional to develop his intuition to the best degree. It can aid your activities to the ultimate degree. You must spend as much time on this as on any other subject you want to learn. Many people train, run, workout, practice karate or martial arts at least one hour a day. Can you imagine how intuitive an individual would be if he intensely practiced sensitivity and psychic ability exercises one hour a day for just six months?

Chapter 19

Manifest Unlimited Creative Consciousness

How do you manifest an unlimited creative consciousness? Let's first consider what would inhibit you from creating this consciousness. The most important element would be how you feel about yourself. If you do not feel very confident, have low self-esteem and don't think you are a valuable person on any level, your outlook would definitely discourage it. Having this attitude would be very hard for you to improve yourself and get a good start.

As mentioned in an earlier chapter, if you talk down to yourself all the time and keep putting yourself down mentally, it would be very hard for you to acquire a strong positive belief in yourself. You wouldn't feel like you could contribute anything to yourself, your family, society, the human race and your friends. This could happen if you had parents who were very negative towards you, didn't encourage you to believe in yourself and kept telling you that you would never make anything of yourself. Being in that atmosphere for so many years usually leaves mental blocks and scars; it usually takes many years to eliminate those mental blocks and feel good. In this case, some may spend their whole lives just trying to find ways to feel better about themselves.

If you have a family, husband, spouse or children around you who don't appreciate you, which can make you feel very unworthy and unvalued. If you have a position in your profession, job or work environment that is negative and un-inspiring, that can add to the trouble. It could be a boss that yells or puts you down every day for everything. There may be work associates there who talk behind each other's back or blame their own faults on other people. You may never get a chance to express yourself or be creative in this sort of work situation. In this case, you could acquire a very resentful attitude from having to be in an environment like this.

In a wider context, someone might live in a country that has a controlling dictator and fundamentalist religious and political beliefs. There may not be any fair law and order existing. It could be a very dangerous country to live in, with people being killed for minor or arbitrary reasons. One of the worst inhibitors of consciousness evolution is living in a country that is poverty-stricken. In the last two situations, you end up focusing all of your energy on ways of just trying to stay alive, keep your family fed and away from being harmed. You and your family are hungry and thirsty all of the time. You are constantly concerned and worried about you or your family running into danger or being killed.

It is extremely hard to be spiritually creative in any of the situations mentioned above. You might become inventive in getting food or money to keep you and your family alive for awhile. It would be very hard to be able to express yourself and acquire an unlimited creative consciousness in any of these situations. By considering many of the situations that would inhibit you from evolving your creative consciousness, you are now able to acquire an idea of what a good atmosphere would be to express yourself.

Basically, you do not want to be around anyone or anything that would inhibit or suppress your actions, thoughts and consciousness. Of course, you still have to stay within the limits of legal and moral laws and that means you can't harm yourself or anyone else. That is also why committing suicide is against the law. It is not just illegal, but in many countries, cultures and religions, it is against mental and spiritual ethics. It is believed that when a person commits suicide he is also killing the God consciousness or creator part of himself. He is basically giving up on his belief of himself and God. This would be the ultimate way to inhibit or suppress your spiritual evolution.

There are exceptions to this though. A warrior or samurai who commits suicide and sacrifices himself for some important cause or belief could liberate many people in the future or in that society. This is a different situation, because of the mentality and the opposite attitude

Gichen Funakoshi, considered the "Father of Modern Day Karate," demonstrating a (shuto-uke) or knife-hand block.

each would have. One individual is depressed, doesn't feel he would make a difference and doesn't even care. He has lost all value for himself. It is a shame, because most of these individuals let themselves get so depressed that they don't realize that they usually leave people behind who care and love them. The depressed person doesn't even care about what his wife, children, family and friends have to go through and live with after he is gone. He is selfish.

The warrior or samurai feels he has lived a purposeful life. He also feels he is dying for a very important cause to help, or liber-

Group photo of prominent karate instructors in 1964, at Ed Parker's first International Tournament in Long Beach. (Left to right, front row: Pat Burleson, Bruce Lee, Anthony Mirakian, Jhoon Rhee. Back row, left to right: Allen Steen, George Mattson, Ed Parker, Tsutomu Ohshima, Robert Trias.)

ate other people. This individual is really sacrificing himself for others. Many soldiers, who fight for the rights of others, also come into this category. When a warrior has these ideals, he trains his whole life with a certain belief and purpose. He has created a reason to be in this physical existence. He has the ability to express himself to an ultimate degree. He can express his unlimited capacities when he dies in battle. This is another elevated example of how you could ultimately express an unlimited free consciousness.

Basically, you are not here on this planet as a physical being having a spiritual experience. Instead, you are here on this planet as a spiritual being having a physical experience. You are not here to be tested. You are here to continually create in a positive, expanding way. The universe is expanding naturally and so is your own consciousness. You are continually creating your own personal universe. You have the soul, choice and ability to bring havoc, problems, and destruction into the universe and various lives, or you can create peace, joy, prosperity and success.

The secret in creating and materializing your dreams and goals lies in taking control of your initial thought process. Whatever you think is also the God conscious part of creating in this universe. Govern, guide and use it well, and you will create the dream universe for yourself.

Tom Muzila visiting Bruce Lee's memorial in the mid-1970's, in Seattle, Washington.

Conclusion

We have been through an incredible amount of material and information. Some of you may be familiar with a certain amount and others may not. As we spoke of in an earlier chapter, it is important to keep an open mind and especially practice the data, information, concepts and exercises. Our minds are quick to analyze and intellectualize information. We think that we understand it. In the eastern mentality of understanding, there are five levels of consciousness, from lower to higher. They consider intelligence as only the second level. In the western understanding, most people put having a higher intelligence on the highest level. It is interesting, because no matter how intelligent a person is, they still can be bias and prejudice. Many intelligent western mentality individual's, only depend on their logic, rational and intelligence to deal with their profession, people and situations in life. This is another major differentiating factor. They have a tendency of not depending much on their physical level. The physical and mental level must work together, as one unit to develop a higher level understanding. A high level idealistic warrior individual would train all of his facets, extremely intense, such as; physical, mental, intellectual and spiritual. He would not just talk and intellectualize the situation, but he is physically doing and experiencing it on every level. For example, if a non-physical, but very intelligent person observed martial artists, or soldiers training beyond all limitations, where it looks like they are torturing themselves? He would probably have a tendency to think they are crazy? This person should not criticize or judge them, because he or she has never experienced what they are doing. Of course, if this person jumps in and attempts to train and experience what these warriors or soldiers are going through and experiencing in this extreme intense training first. After they actually experienced that situation, they will have a much better objective mentality to make an opinion or criticism. It is more evolved and objective, to experience a certain situation or atmosphere, before you comment on it.